IMAGES
of America

NEW CASTLE COUNTY POLICE DEPARTMENT

On the Cover: The cover photograph is of the first class of County Rural Police Officers. A one-month academy was mandated by Levy Court in 1930, the year these officers graduated. As conservators of peace, they were responsible for enforcing laws and regulations under Levy Court jurisdiction. These were the first of what would become the New Castle County Police Department. (Courtesy of the New Castle County Police Department archives.)

IMAGES of America

NEW CASTLE COUNTY POLICE DEPARTMENT

New Castle County Police Department

Foreword by Thomas P. Gordon

ARCADIA PUBLISHING

ISBN 978-0-7385-9928-1

Published by Arcadia Publishing
Charleston, South Carolina

Printed in the United States of America

Library of Congress Control Number: 2012955052

For all general information, please contact Arcadia Publishing:
Telephone 843-853-2070
Fax 843-853-0044
E-mail sales@arcadiapublishing.com
For customer service and orders:
Toll-Free 1-888-313-2665

Visit us on the Internet at www.arcadiapublishing.com

This book is dedicated to the men and women of the New Castle County Police Department, past, present, and future.

Contents

Foreword

On behalf of the citizens of New Castle County and the men and women of the New Castle County government, we congratulate the New Castle County Police Department on its 100th anniversary. I salute all of the officers, past and present, for making this department one of the best in the United States.

I had the privilege of serving as both your police chief and county executive. Together, we were able to transform the agency into a world-class example of community policing, which it still is today.

As we enter our agency's second century, we call upon all of our extended family for support; together, we can continue the progress.

—Thomas P. Gordon
New Castle County Executive

ACKNOWLEDGMENTS

The authors would like to acknowledge all the men and women who have served and those that will continue to serve this agency with dedication and pride. It is the faces of these brave men and women that appear in the 100 years of photographs proudly serving the communities of New Castle County. We would like to thank the New Castle County government and Police Command staff for their approval of this project. To the members of the 100th anniversary committee, thank you for your countless hours of determination in paying tribute to this great time in New Castle County Police history.

There have been many involved in this process, but special thanks are given to the authors: Det. Melissa Bell, Cpl. John Weglarz, Officer First Class Annette Irons, Senior Lt. Laura O'Sullivan, and Capt. Wendi Feeser. Additionally, Retired Senior Cpl. Trinidad Navarro, Retired Capt. George Williamson, Retired Senior Sgt. David Stewart, Retired Senior Sgt. James Leonard, Retired Senior Sgt. Robert Larrimore, Retired Senior Cpl. Edward Sommers, Retired Cpl. John Krzysiak, and Senior Cpl. Albert Wysock have provided photographs, knowledge, and history of the department that were vital to the making of this publication. Photographer John Randolph also provided photographs of the New Castle County Police Headquarters and Academy.

Unless otherwise noted, all photographs are courtesy of the New Castle County Police Department archives.

INTRODUCTION

Delaware is the second-smallest state in the union, with an area of 2,306 square miles. It ranks 45th in population, with approximately 897, 934 people in 2010. New Castle County was formed by a land grant for William Penn in 1767. It occupies about one-fifth of the state's area (437 square miles), but it contains two-thirds of the population (510,000). The state is still divided into hundreds (from an old Anglo-Saxon term for districts with governing responsibilities), but they have lost all of their political functions and linger today only as geographical designations. In Delaware, the hundred described an area in which 100 white men live. The state has 38 hundreds, 11 of which are in New Castle County. The county has 16 incorporated cities or towns, 5 of which have their own local police forces, and 17 unincorporated cities and towns.

Many institutions of government were brought over from the old country, be it from the Netherlands, Sweden, or England. The Levy Court was established by the Dutch in the mid-1600s for the purpose of tax control and collection, but grew to become the system of government for Delaware's counties. Constables were appointed to assist the court, and their duties were expanded as the functions of the court grew. The Levy Court system of governance existed in New Castle County until 1965, in Sussex County until 1969, and it still exists in Kent County.

The constabulary was an institution brought over from England. The constable, elected from among the overseers of the town or parish, made tax assessments and collections. He was relied upon to enforce laws known as the Duke of York Laws. He was also responsible for the pursuit and apprehension of offenders, including the organization of others to assist. He would take violators into custody and keep them under lock and key until arraignment before a judge of the peace, who traveled throughout the area. This could take days, weeks, or months. His badge was a six-foot-long staff emblazoned with the king's coat of arms, which he could not act without and which was a symbol of the constable's power and authority.

After 1770, the Court of General Appeals appointed at least one constable for each hundred, and, after 1832, the Levy Court made the appointments. Duties, some of which continue to this day, included the execution of court orders, warrants, and processes. He ensured the peace of the state by enforcing its laws, and arrested those committing riot, murder, theft, or breach of peace. The constabulary remained as the law enforcement agency for New Castle County until 1911, when Levy Court was authorized to appoint two officers with responsibility for enforcing the largest community complaint: automobile traffic violations.

Also in 1911, the Levy Court authorized the establishment of the County Rural Police, with two police officers each for the Brandywine Hundred and the Christiana Hundred. In each hundred, one officer was to be a Republican, the other a Democrat, and they had to reside in the hundred they represented. Public pressure forced compliance with this law and the appointment of officers. In January 1912, a petition was signed by the residents of the Brandywine Hundred requesting compliance with the 1911 legislation. The residents of the Christiana Hundred signed the same petition in February of that year. Daniel Knight, the first elected officer, made a salary of $730 a year, or $2 per day. He was the first County Rural Police Officer, which was the predecessor to today's New Castle County Police Department.

Later in 1912, another county police agency, the County Highway Police, was formed. The agencies were separate in their duties but eventually came to represent the beginnings of the New Castle County Police Department.

Two men, Charles Bowers and Fred T. Fleetwood, were duly appointed in December 1913 and became the nucleus of the County Highway Police, also known as the County Auto Police. They attended a one-month police academy and were given a salary of $1,800 a year. The force evolved into a small—10-man—but relatively efficient police force by the early 1920s. Each man was issued his own Harley-Davidson Model 74. His issued equipment included shirts, trousers, leather jackets, leggings, shoes, a hat, a tie, a .38 caliber six-inch-barrel Colt revolver, and handcuffs. They used key clocks throughout the county and would check in once an hour. The first four-wheel patrol vehicle was a Ford Model A panel truck, which was utilized during the midnight shift.

The Rural Police remained a token force behind the Highway Police until the latter was abolished in 1935, when the State Highway Patrol took over responsibility for the patrolling of all roadways in the state. Five of the County Highway Police Officers were hired by the new agency.

In the 1930s, Levy Court authorized Rural Police authority in all of New Castle County. It also mandated that all officers must attend a one-month academy.

Over the ensuing years, the law was amended to provided additional police officers: in 1937, four for each Brandywine Hundred and Christiana Hundred; in 1939, four for New Castle Hundred; in 1953, four for Mill Creek Hundred; and in 1955, officers for each of the six remaining hundreds. Until 1951, the officers were required to stay in the hundred they were assigned to during the tour of duty. The law was again amended to allow officers to exercise powers in any of the hundreds authorized to have Rural Police. This provided more manpower to hundreds that were in need of extra policing and allowed officers to assist each other in patrol and investigations.

In 1965, there was a complete revision of Delaware law pertaining to the police. The designated manpower allocations were dropped, as were residency requirements and political affiliations. The hundreds were no longer required to have equal Democratic and Republican officers, and officers were not required to live within the hundred that they patrolled. Also in 1965, a director was named and the official title of the force was changed to the New Castle County Police Department.

The New Castle County Police Department survived abolishment movements several times, and, in the 1970s, a jurisdictional agreement with the Delaware State Police was enacted. This jurisdictional agreement remains in place today. The department maintains jurisdictional agreements with other local agencies within New Castle County as well, and often assists other agencies when needed.

The New Castle County Police Department grew from a small traditional force of 22 men to the second-largest police agency in the state, with approximately 350 sworn officers trained and dedicated to "excellence in policing." The department is staffed by a chief of police, majors, captains, lieutenants, sergeants, corporals, and police officers. Officers are now equipped with a take-home vehicle and laptop, which has forever changed the way policing is done. Quick identification and automated ticketing and summonses allows for officers to stay within the communities during their shifts.

There are numerous specialized units in the department, which allows for many career opportunities, including the criminal investigations unit and the special operations unit. Career development is important for the process of mentoring and developing the future leaders of the department. The department searches for the best training and schools to develop both officers and supervisors.

The stated mission of the department "is to improve the quality of life throughout New Castle County by striving to provide a secure community environment through the delivery of police service in an efficient manner." Recognizing the importance of police-community relations in accomplishing this mission, the New Castle County Police Department has committed itself to community-oriented policing.

Community-oriented policing has taken on many different approaches throughout the years, but the essence has always been to provide excellent service to the citizens of New Castle County. The department has utilized community watch programs, problem-oriented policing, and intelligence-led policing. Recently, the department has begun utilizing predictive policing to combat crime. Crime clearance rates have traditionally been well above the national average in New Castle County. The increased ability to solve crimes can be credited to the many approaches used to combat changing crime trends.

The department takes great pride in being a leader in technology and new policing philosophies. With the technologically savvy world we live in, criminals have also gotten more advanced. Grant funding on local, state, and federal levels allow the department to purchase the most up-to-date equipment. The same funding is also used to fund overtime assignments in problem areas. To ensure the department communicates and shares resources on a daily basis, an internal website, *Portal*, was created. Portal acts as our internal newspaper and blog, and has assisted in solving numerous crimes. Even with the recent economic downfall, the department has found a way to grow and flourish.

Throughout history, the New Castle County Police Department has experienced challenges, successes, and a few growing pains. Yet, the department has kept in step with the community. The growth of New Castle County will continue to drive the force forward, without ever losing sight of those who helped create the department.

The brave men and women of the department prepare for work each day with the protection and service of the community in their minds. From their uniform presentation to their public interaction to engaging with violent suspects, New Castle County police officers face a variety of incidents in any given workday. Their professionalism and willingness to face danger is a point of pride for everyone who dons the badge of a police officer, but is especially true of the men and woman who serve with the New Castle County Police Department.

One

UNIFORMS

The first level of control officers have in any situation is their mere presence. Immediately, the citizens around them will look at them and judge their character and ability to police by the way that they appear. The New Castle County Police Department has worked through its history to always have uniforms that conveyed a commanding presence and authority.

In December 1913, the first officers of the Rural Police were issued shirts, trousers, leather jackets, leggings, shoes, a hat, a tie, a .38 caliber six-inch-barrel Colt revolver, and handcuffs. The idea behind any police uniform is to be readily identified as an authoritative presence upon arrival. Police uniforms were originally patterned off of military uniforms, as they were seen as people in authority. During this time, there was little money available for uniforms. Therefore, three to four different uniforms were known to be worn at one time as a cost-saving measure. The uniforms were a mixture of military green and dark blue. The guns were positioned for cross-draw to allow for easy access within the constraints of the early modes of transportation. The officer seen here wears boots and britches, which were phased out but are now within regulation.

This photograph was taken in McDaniel Crest in the 1950s. The Rural Police officer wears a blue eight-pointed hat. The uniform consists of green pants with a blue stripe and a blue jacket. The gun has been moved from cross-draw to a strong-side draw. During the winter months, blouse-style jackets were worn by patrolmen while on duty. (Courtesy of Retired Senior Cpl. Albert Wysock.)

The Eisenhower jacket was a waistcoat that was worn during the spring, summer, and fall. This is another example of police uniforms mimicking military styles. This photograph was taken with a telephoto lens as the Rural Police assisted the Delaware State Police on a manhunt for a suspect that shot a state police detective. The manhunt occurred in the area of Delaware Route 273 and US Route 13.

Throughout the New Castle County Police Department's history, there have been many uniform changes, which have been brought about for several different reasons. These ranged from a change in chief to a lack of a consistent clothing vendor to a change in policing. Changes are seen through the next several photographs. This photograph was taken between 1965 and 1967 and shows half of the Rural Police force. The hat has gone from a small-billed brim hat that could be worn while riding a motorcycle to a larger, campaign-style hat. The larger hat was brought into service when vehicles were becoming the main mode of transportation. They went from a small circular-style hat to a straw Stetson-style hat for the hotter weather. Felt Stetsons eventually followed, and they were followed by the brown campaign hat.

The New Castle County Police always wore darker clothing that was sometimes mixed with lighter. The colors ranged from blue to green to khaki to brown, which is worn now. This photograph was taken in 1968 or 1969. Because there were times when quick recognition of rank was needed, white shirts were worn by those with the rank of lieutenant and above.

The 1970s brought more changes in uniform. The color scheme was inverted, and the officers now wore dark colors on the top and lighter colors on the bottom. Prior to this time, blue was always incorporated into the uniform. Now, the uniform was what has become known as "county brown." This color change distinguished the New Castle County Police Department from other departments within the state of Delaware.

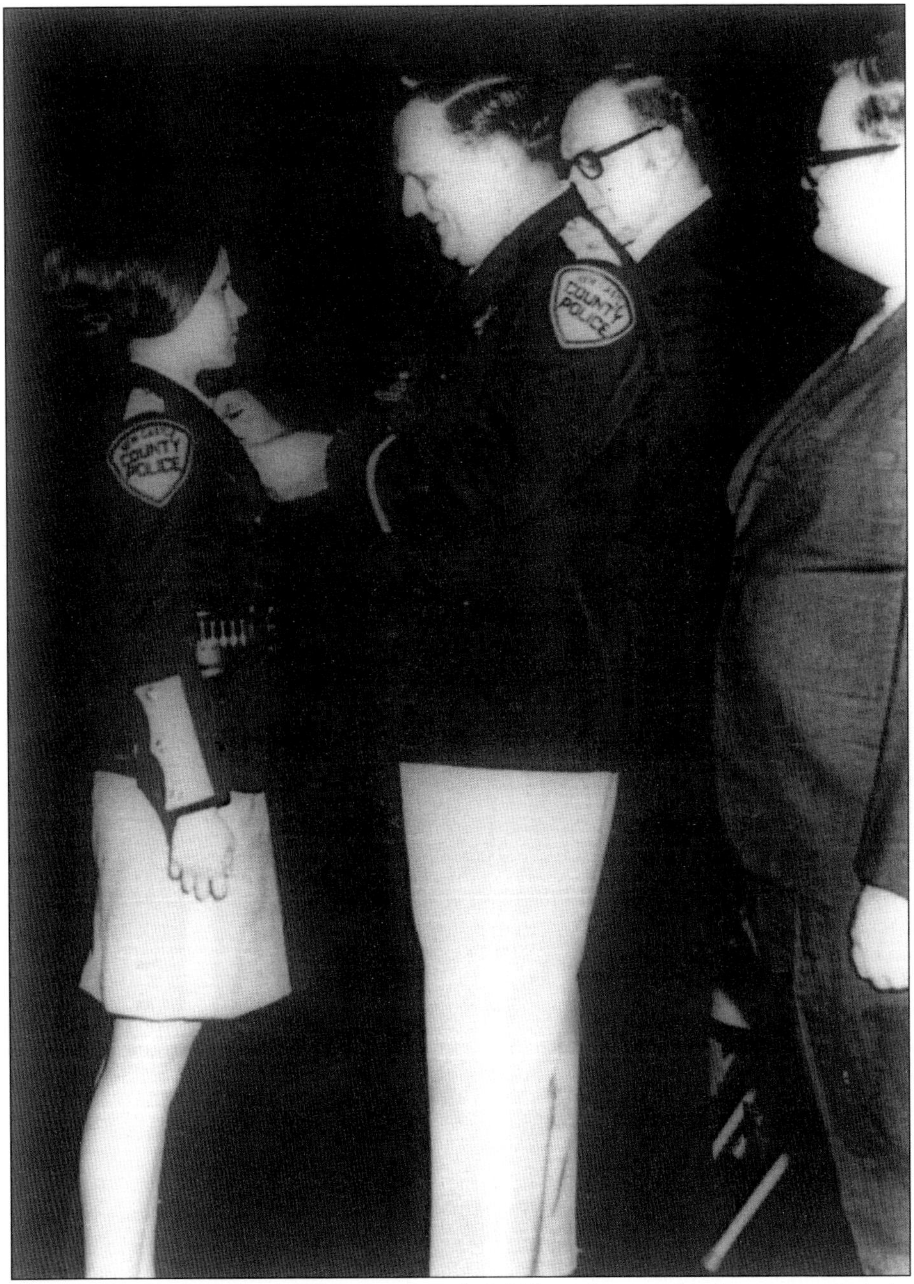

Pants, which started out as tight-fitting, were styled differently once the department switched to motor vehicles from motorcycles. These pants allowed better movement in and out of the vehicles. In 1972, the first female officer, Jeanette M. Lloyd, was hired. As evidenced by the photograph, Officer Lloyd's uniform was originally a skirt and blouse coat. The next two academy classes after Jeannette Lloyd also required female officers to wear the skirt for all day-work tours. During the night tour, female officers were allowed to wear pants similar to the male officers' uniform pants. A short time later, the female officers' uniform was changed to conform to the male officers' uniform, substituting the skirt for pants on all shifts. While the uniforms were originally tailored for men, there are now more companies that specialize in uniforms tailored to fit women better.

In the 1970s, the New Castle County Police Department hired cadets, people who had an interest in pursuing a law enforcement career, particularly with the New Castle County Police. Candidates were under the age of 21 and worked out of headquarters. They were used for several different tasks, including fueling vehicles and helping the on-duty commander. They also were tasked with patrolling the New Castle County parklands, and had arrest powers within the parks. They wore khaki uniforms that mimicked the sworn personnel's uniform and patch. There was a special cadet badge that was issued to each cadet as well. Due to changing times, the practice of hiring cadets has been abandoned. However, some recruit officers are hired prior to starting at the academy, and they perform functions similar to what the previous cadets were tasked to do. A badge is no longer issued, and recruits do not have arrest powers.

In 1982, the New Castle County Police Department won an Outstanding Achievement Award in the best-dressed competition. The uniform consisted of tan pants with a gold stripe running down the outside leg seam. The top was a dark brown shirt that was made in short or long sleeves to accommodate weather conditions. The New Castle County Police Department still issues a summer and a winter uniform for officer comfort. The switch to the new seasonal uniform is done department-wide to ensure that everyone is identically dressed. The change to the summer uniform is usually done shortly after National Law Enforcement Memorial Week in May. The change to the winter uniform usually occurs in late October. In 1988, body armor was issued to all officers. Worn under the uniform shirt, the vest not only protects officers from gunfire and serious assaults but also helps with impacts from motor vehicle collisions.

In the late 20th century, uniforms for specialized units began to change in order to increase mobility, visibility, and safety. Today, there are a variety of police uniforms and the styles vary depending on the assignment. For example, the bicycle unit now has pants or shorts to choose from, depending on the weather.

This photograph was taken in December 2012 and represents all of the uniforms of the New Castle County Police Department. The uniforms have evolved over the years, but have always maintained a professional appearance. These uniforms range from bright, visible colors to tactical dark colors. When each officer puts on his or her uniform for a shift, it represents not only personal pride but also pride in the department.

The New Castle County Rural Police patch was the first patch known to be worn on a uniform. It was worn from the 1940s to the early-to-mid-1960s. The patch (above) was dark blue in color, with yellow facing and yellow writing. It was worn on both shoulders of the shirts and jackets in both winter and summer. The New Castle County Police patch (below) was only worn on the reefer jacket, a blue military-style jacket that was worn by the Rural Police in harsh winter weather. This patch was reversed in the late 1960s and 1970s, with yellow becoming the dominant color, and the piping being blue, and later brown.

The Levy Court of New Castle County patch (right) was worn from the mid-1960s until the mid-1970s. It is a very light blue patch with yellow accents. The middle of the patch represents industry and agriculture specific to New Castle County. When the uniforms switched to "county brown," the piping on the patch also changed to brown to match. There were several other variations of patches through the ensuing years. The current patch (below) came in 1996. An officer took on the task of designing it, and kept the water features and castle but added "New Castle County, 1673, Delaware" to the middle.

The New Castle County Auxiliary Police patch (above) was worn in the 1950s and 1960s, along with a Civil Defense badge. This group was made up of retired police officers and civilians who assisted the police with traffic on accident scenes. This particular duty is now carried out by fire police. However, the idea continues today with the V.I.P. program, in which retired officers and civilian volunteers work assisting specialized units. The cadet patch (below) was worn by cadets to differentiate them from sworn officers. When they were sent to patrol New Castle County parks, they needed a uniform to assert authority.

Specialized units began to adopt patches to recognize the officer's participation. These smaller patches, seen above and at right, were worn on the right forearm, as to not interfere with the coveted service stripes on the left forearm. Each service stripe indicates three years of service. The smaller specialized patches included motorcycle officers, the Honor Guard, the Mounted Unit, and the Canine Unit. Due to their expense, these patches have been discontinued and replaced by unit pins that are worn above the right breast pocket. Some larger unit patches remain in use, and shoulder patches still exist for the canine and SWAT teams.

In addition to patches, pins, and badges, rank insignia is also worn on the uniform. For the first three years of service, the officer is known as a "slick sleeve," meaning that he or she has no service stripes or rank insignia. After completing three years of service, the officer gets the title of officer first class and receives a single gold rocker, as seen above at upper left, to place on both sleeves under the county patch. After 12 years of service, a second rocker is added, making the rank of corporal. After another four years, the title of senior corporal is earned, marked by a bottom rocker. Officers must test for sergeant, and can then be awarded the three stripes. Staff officers are considered to be the rank of lieutenant and above. As seen below, single gold bars indicate lieutenant, double bars indicate captain, the oak leaf indicates major, and the eagle indicates colonel.

Back in the days of the "shire reeve," the precursor to the modern sheriff in England, the shire reeve and his "hundreds," or officers, wore a plate in the shape of a five-, six-, or seven-point star made of brass, metal, or any other material that could be highly polished and visible by moonlight. This allowed them to identify each other; over time, they began to put markings and insignias on the plates. This developed into common practice, and when the first formal, paid, uniformed police department was established in New York in the 1850s, they wore badges, as they had become known. The first New Castle County badge is shown at right. These badges included badge numbers to identify officers. The badge below was the second badge used, which combined a badge shape with the sheriff-style star.

A police badge is usually in the shape of a shield, symbolizing the police officer as a protector of the peace and of the people. It is tradition for uniformed officers to wear their badges on the left side of their chests. It is placed over the heart and is symbolic of the oath and pledge the officers take.

Identifying the specific county became important as the population of Delaware grew. The New Castle County Police Department, the only county police department in Delaware, wanted its authority to be recognized. Surrounding states also had county and municipal departments, so it became more important to differentiate which county the officer was employed by. The badge color was silver throughout these years, and continued to include badge numbers.

No rank was associated with the badges, which eventually grew in size from the original issue, approximately one inch in size, to approximately two inches in size. Another badge worn by officers was the gold Levy Court badge, a circular badge that paid homage to the Levy Court and Rural Police titles.

Through the history of the New Castle County Police Department, the title with which officers were addressed also changed. The patrolman eventually became an officer. Rank for supervisors was also displayed on the top portion of the badge, which was originally silver in color, with a gold circle in the middle displaying the county patch features.

In the 1990s, the badge was changed over to gold for the entire department. The title on the badge also changes with rank. The ranks of officer and officer first class have badges that indicate "officer," and so on. The latest gold badge has now incorporated the newer New Castle County logo in the center.

The New Castle County Police Department is extremely proud to be celebrating 100 years of policing the citizens of New Castle County. The 100th Anniversary Committee was formed to ensure that this memorable time in history would not be forgotten. The committee designed the 100th anniversary patch seen here, which incorporates old with new. The same was done for the 100th anniversary badge.

A handgun is one of the most important parts of a police officer's uniform. Most officers go their entire careers without needing to fire their guns outside of the police range. One of the first issued handguns was the Colt "Official Police" .38 special. This handgun was a six-shot revolver, and extra ammunition was carried as individually holstered bullets, making reloading the gun a slow process. On the bottom of the handgun was a small latch, which connected a piece of leather from the handgun to the epaulette. Holsters were not tight-fitting, which kept the handgun from falling out. Prior to this weapon being issued to New Castle County police officers, they were required to purchase their own. Today, officers are issued their weapons, which are carried on duty and can also be carried off duty.

The department regulates off-duty weapons and maintains a list of preapproved guns that can be carried. All officers must qualify with these weapons after they are approved and inspected by the range master. This regulates the caliber and ensures familiarity with the weapon, in case its use is called upon off duty in a stressful situation. These weapons vary from semiautomatic weapons to revolvers. This handgun is a Smith & Wesson Model 10, a blue steel six-shot revolver. The blue steel helps keep a cleaner appearance and prevents rust. Traditionally, officers keep their weapons in clean working order to ensure their readiness. Inspections ensure that officers maintain their weapons and other equipment. Speed loaders were eventually introduced to assist in reloading weapons more quickly and were carried in a holster-like compartment on the duty belt.

Officers are required to qualify for their handguns with two daytime qualification courses and one nighttime qualification course each year. Officers who carry specialized firearms such as rifles and shotguns must also meet the same requirements with their specific firearm. Above is a Smith & Wesson Model 64 six-shot revolver. In the late 1980s, the department switched to a semiautomatic nine-millimeter handgun made by Smith & Wesson. There were several changes in nine-millimeter models over the next decade. In the 1990s, the department used the Smith & Wesson Model 5946 double-action nine-millimeter handgun. Seen below, it was the first double-action handgun used by the department.

In the 2000s, the New Castle County Police Department switched handguns again, to the Smith & Wesson Model M&P nine-millimeter (above). This gun was much lighter than the all-steel Model 5946. The new M&P also had increased magazine size, allowing for more ammunition to be carried by an officer. The department also began issuing AR-15 rifles in the 2000s. The department did not have enough rifles to issue to every patrol officer, however, and many officers began purchasing their own rifles. Below are two officers who purchased their own rifles to carry on routine patrol.

Two

VEHICLES

The department's first official vehicle was a motorcycle. The first four-wheeled vehicle was a Ford Model T, which was only to be used on the midnight shift. Eventually, automobiles became the main mode of transportation for officers. The department has grown to have the ability to assign a vehicle to every officer, and it is also supplemented by specialty vehicles.

In the early 1900s, the first motorcycles used by the New Castle County Police Department were manufactured by Harley-Davidson. Police departments found that motorcycles were an inexpensive means of responding to crimes and controlling traffic. Originally, there were no stop signs, speed limits, or even basic rules of the road. Roads, if they existed, were not good in the early 1900s, and travel was difficult by any mode of transportation. Motorcycles were ridden year-round in all kinds of weather. The motorcycles were sparsely equipped, and the men who rode them were rugged pioneers paving the way for future law enforcement officers. The original motorcycles were generally a darker color like brown or blue, but later they all became white, which helped with visibility and made all the colors uniform.

Time and technology have greatly changed the look and use of motorcycles used by the New Castle County Police Department. Today, the department utilizes all Harley-Davidson motorcycles, equipped with lights, sirens, radios, and some even with laptops and Bluetooth printers. The maneuverability of the motorcycle offers huge advantages over traditional police vehicles. The department has numerous officers trained to ride motorcycles, and they have been effectively used by the Traffic Services Unit for traffic enforcement. Motorcycles are not used as the primary means of transportation for the officers on a daily basis, but are used for special events such as parades, escorts of dignitaries, funeral processions, and other traffic functions. Since Joe Biden, who lives in Delaware, became vice president in 2008, the motorcycles have been used more frequently in the vice presidential motorcade with the Secret Service.

In the late 1960s, the New Castle County Police Department's vehicles were powder blue in color. A 1968 Chevrolet Biscayne is seen here. A new phone number, 737-7000, was assigned to the county police and marked on all police vehicles, along with the latest reflector tape, bar lights, and alley lights. Other departments referred to the police vehicles as "circus wagons" and said the high visibility would not work—that it would instead alert criminals of their arrival. Today, it has been proven to be the best thing to have happened to police cars in terms of safety. While stealth movements are sometimes necessary in police work, officers often conduct vehicle stops on well-traveled roads. Having several visual indicators on the patrol vehicle alerts other drivers to slow down and be cautious near the stop.

Changing times brought about different makes, models, and colors of vehicles to the department. Seen here is a 1968 Chevrolet station wagon that is dark blue in color with white doors and sparse identification insignia. It was used by the Traffic Unit because it was one of the few cars big enough to carry around the equipment needed at accident scenes. In 1973, the department added a Plymouth Fury to the fleet. It was one of the first dark brown vehicles used by the department. Officers who have driven the vehicle remark that it was one of the fastest police vehicles built. The light bars changed several times through the years, from the first bars with one single-colored light to today's bar, with numerous tricolored LED lights for safety and visibility.

This photograph was taken in downtown Wilmington at a parade. The dark brown vehicles continued into the 1970s with these 1977 Plymouth Satellites, which each sported a gold roof and gold stripping. The color scheme distinguished them from other police agencies in the area. The only department insignias on the vehicles were a door seal on the driver's side and passenger's side doors. During these times, vehicle safety was not at the forefront, and seat belt use was minimal. Today, safety is a huge concern because of the higher speeds and technology distractions in cars. The safety of the officer and the prisoners are now considered top priorities when selecting new vehicles for the fleet. With the approach of the 100th anniversary, the department is considering going back in history to the more traditional dark-colored, marked police cars. (Courtesy of John Randolph.)

The Chevrolet Caprice Classic was added to the fleet in the mid-1970s. This vehicle was left unmarked and used for traffic enforcement details. The unmarked cars are seen as more stealthy and blend in with other vehicles on the street, to enhance the officer's ability to get an accurate sense for how people truly drive within the communities. Unmarked cars were also utilized to make moving around the communities easier for detectives who were not responding to active 911 complaints. While the majority of the fleet consists of marked vehicles, the purchase of unmarked vehicles continues. Through the years, unmarked cars have included Ford Crown Victorias, Dodge Durangos, Ford Expeditions, Chevrolet Tahoes, and other vehicles. Some of these unmarked vehicles are utilized on the street by specialized units while others are used by staff officers.

In the 1980s, the vehicles of choice were the Chevrolet Caprice Classic (above) and the Dodge Diplomat (below). Once again, the paint scheme changed, with the vehicle remaining dark brown, but with a white roof and white stripping. The Caprice Classic was assigned to the town of Middletown, as designated by the markings on the vehicle. Two officers per shift were assigned to patrol Middletown. To ensure residents that the officers were not just driving through, the vehicles were specifically marked "Middletown Patrol." Huge advances to the light bars and equipment in the vehicles were just around the corner.

The 1990s brought about the first batch of white vehicles, which were chosen to make the police vehicles more visible to the public. It also ensured a color continuity of vehicles for the years to come. Many vehicle manufacturers slightly alter their brown or tan color each year, leaving a department with slightly different shades of colors. However, there are no differences in white from year to year. The brand-new Ford Crown Victorias seen here had the most up-to-date equipment available. The cars were the beginning of an image that has remained with the New Castle County Police Department. In 1991, the department won a vehicle design contest sponsored by *Law and Order* magazine.

In 1997, the New Castle County Police Department issued each officer a take-home vehicle, which brought about change to the agency. It was believed that officers would respond to incidents on the way to and from work, which was proven correct and still occurs on a daily basis. Off-duty officers rather frequently respond to thousands of calls for service that would have normally waited for an on-duty unit to handle. Officers were also more visible in the communities in which they resided, a part of the department known as the Community Enhancement Program. Additionally, assigning vehicles to officers allowed the vehicles to last longer in the fleet, since they were not running 24 hours a day. It is the officer's responsibility to make certain that preventative maintenance is performed on the vehicles to ensure that they last longer within the fleet.

The agency continued to add Ford Crown Victorias to the department's fleet throughout the 1990s and 2000s. Snow, hurricanes, and other severe weather conditions also brought about the need for four-wheel-drive vehicles. Ford Explorers, Chevrolet Blazers, Dodge Durangos, and Chevrolet Tahoes were eventually added to the department's fleet. Most of the sport-utility vehicles were assigned to supervisors or SWAT team members, and none were given to routine patrol officers. The extra storage space in these larger vehicles allowed SWAT members to have their equipment in the field, allowing for quicker responses to emergency situations. In severe weather conditions, sport-utility vehicles had to be recalled and assigned to the patrol division for normal patrol functions. Technology has made a huge impact on vehicles and their uses, as different models and types enable more storage and specialized equipment to be installed to assist officers on a daily basis.

In 2011, Ford made the last model year of the Crown Victoria, which had a significant impact on many police departments, which began searching for replacements. The New Castle County Police Department has piloted the Chevrolet Caprice and is currently in the pilot process with the Ford Interceptor Sedan (above) and Interceptor Utility (below). The department continues to search for a car that can comfortably accommodate all the necessary equipment and the officer. In 2012, there was also a proposed change to the graphics package on the department's vehicles, as seen on both of these vehicles.

The mid-1970s International pickup truck above was assigned to park security. During the 1975 recession, a federal program was started that allowed for the hiring of eight park security officers. They had no arrest powers, and their primary functions were to open gates and bathrooms in the parks. In 1979, the program was discontinued and the officers were either brought on as police officers or laid off. The bus below, donated by the National Guard, was used to transport officers to incidents that arose during desegregation. On the bus's first outing, it broke down on the St. Georges Bridge.

In addition to marked patrol vehicles, the New Castle County Police Department maintains unmarked detective cars and numerous specialty vehicles in the fleet. The Canine Unit was started in 1986 with one officer and a bloodhound. In the past, Caprice Classic vehicles were used. Today, the Canine Units carry additional equipment, and the department has learned that sport-utility vehicles are a better fit for the unit. (Courtesy of Officer First Class Steven Donahue.)

The New Castle County Police Department has a long history and reputation for using community policing. The Crime Prevention Unit, established in 1976 and later renamed the Community Services Unit, used this utility vehicle. The officers assigned to this unit concentrated on issues like burglary prevention, residential security, and crime prevention checks.

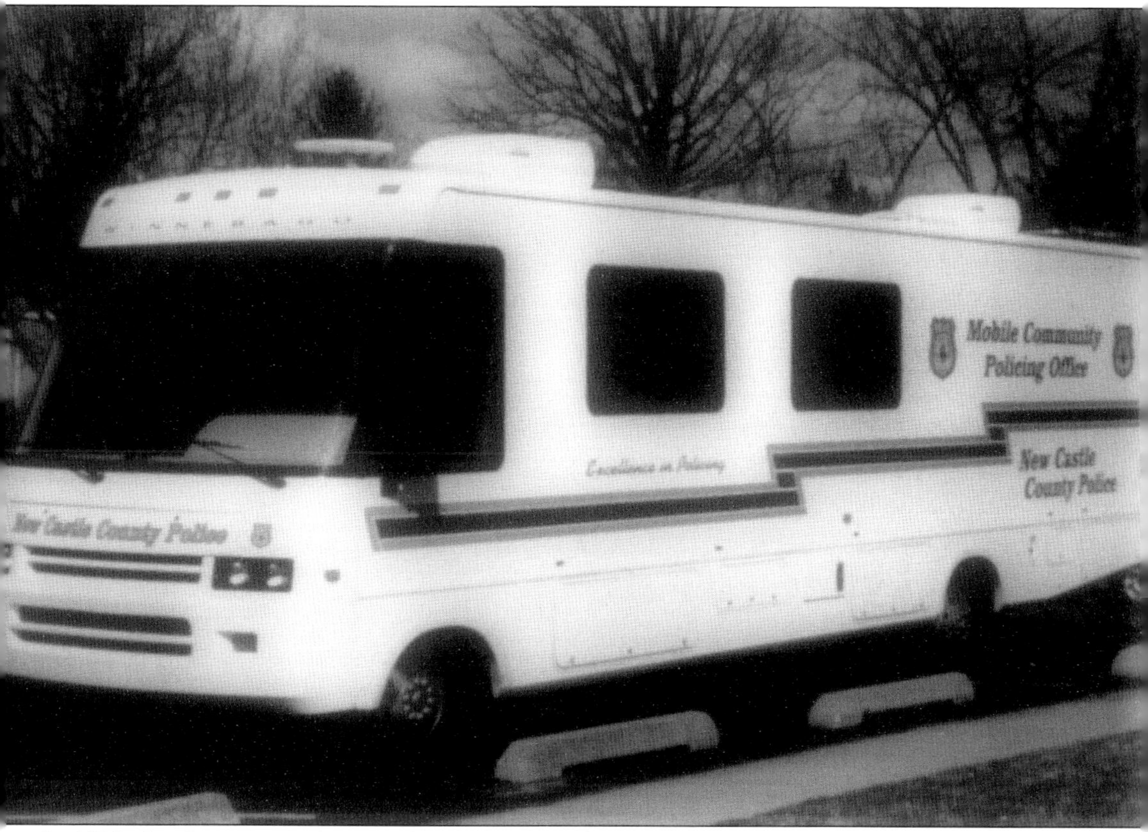

In 1989, the Community Services Unit was pressed into a more proactive role after the more advanced and technological Mobile Community Policing Office was purchased. This vehicle was deployed to communities for events and was highly visible. It allowed for the easy transport of equipment used for community programs such as Child ID, where children are fingerprinted for identification in case they go missing. This vehicle has since been taken out of service, replaced by smaller, easily maneuverable sport-utility vehicles. However, nothing can replace the visibility of this unit when it pulled into an event. Similar vehicles are used by other public safety divisions such as the Emergency Services Department and the Communications Department, to serve as a mobile hospital and a communications center respectively. The police department has access to these vehicles and can have them respond to scenes as required.

The Special Weapons and Tactics Unit (SWAT) provides a well disciplined and highly trained response to situations where the public and/or officers are in extreme danger and at a distinct disadvantage. Due to these types of responses, the SWAT team requires specialized vehicles. The box truck above allows for the transportation of team members and equipment to scenes. The truck is in a constant state of readiness. The department's Lenco vehicle (below) is a tactical armored security vehicle utilized by the SWAT team in many situations. The Lenco has been a key factor in many successful resolutions. (Below, courtesy of Officer Eric Godwin.)

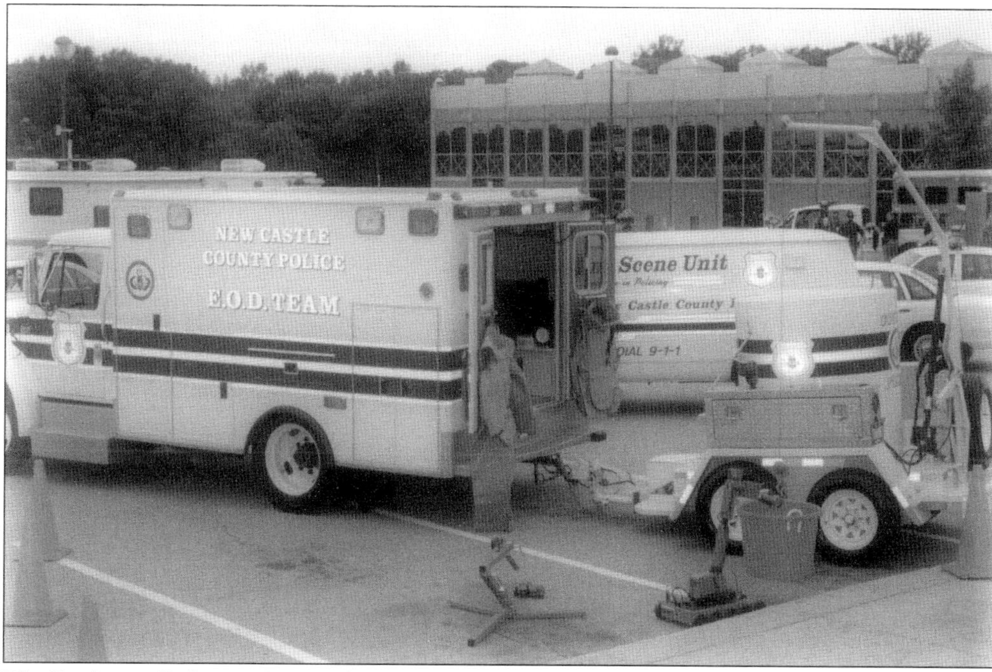

The Explosive Ordnance Disposal (EOD) team is on call 24 hours a day and usually responds with the SWAT team. The technicians are highly trained and require very sophisticated equipment. The EOD vehicle (above) is utilized on call outs. It can house the robot assigned to the unit, as well as many other items. The New Castle County Crisis Negotiation team is also on call 24 hours a day. The team works in conjunction with the SWAT team to safely resolve critical incidents, which include barricaded subjects, hostage situations, and other high-risk services. The Crisis Negotiation team vehicle (below) transports all of the team's specialized equipment.

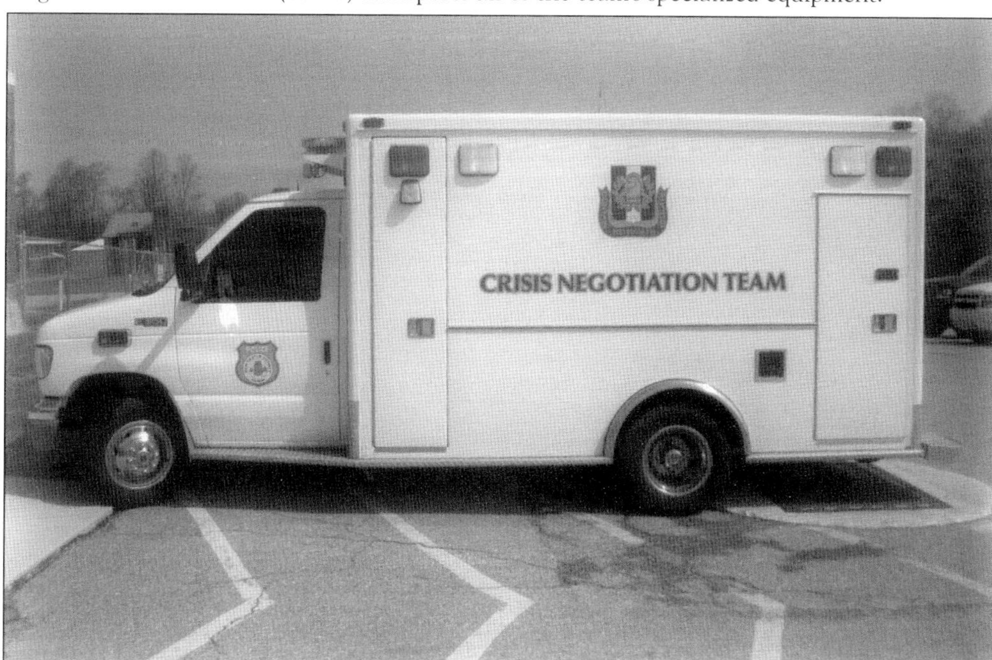

The New Castle County Police Mounted Patrol Unit was formed in 1981 and has been a long-standing tradition. The unit has received countless awards in national competitions. The Ford truck (above) is used to trailer the mounts from community to community. The unit has also added ATVs to the fleet. These specialized vehicles (below) are used to patrol parks and communities. Both the horses and the ATVs attract a lot of attention when they are used on patrol. The officers assigned to the unit are highly trained riders in both modes of transportation.

The Evidence Detection Unit is made up of highly trained detectives that are responsible for the processing of crime scenes. The unit is routinely called out to investigate crimes of a very serious nature. One of the first Evidence Detection Unit vans is seen here, in a time when officers and detectives were not permitted to take vehicles home. Detectives responded to headquarters to pick up the Evidence Detection Unit and then responded to the crime scene. Today, the Evidence Detection technicians are usually assigned a sport-utility vehicle, so they always have their equipment available. Most of these vehicles are unmarked and vary in color and style. Because they have more computerized equipment, ladders, and specialized tools, more space is needed. A converted Explosive Ordnance Destruction vehicle is now utilized to transport equipment to larger, extensive crime scenes.

In 2012, the department obtained three surplus military-grade Humvees, which are currently in the process of being converted into marked patrol vehicles. They will be ready for routine use during inclement weather. The Humvee is known for its ability to travel through deep snow and high water. New Castle County experiences these weather conditions infrequently, but, when they do occur, they require immediate police responses. Four officers can be easily transported in this vehicle, along with all of their equipment and other weather-related equipment. The department has collaborated with the National Guard to provide officers with special training to operate this vehicle. The department also plans to utilize the Humvees for recruiting and special events. It its short time with the department, the Humvee has drawn a lot of attention from citizens and the department's own officers, who are anxious for the opportunity to get a look at the Humvee.

Three

BUILDINGS

The New Castle County Police Department has moved several times in its first 100 years. The department strives to make sure that communities feel they have a police presence in them, so it works out of several small community patrol stations like this one, while keeping its headquarters in a central location near the New Castle County government.

As time went on, centralization became an important factor in New Castle County government. A location was sought to house most public safety entities in a good area. That place was found with the New Castle County Engineering Building, seen above and below, at 2701 Kirkwood Highway. This building brought together the police department, emergency medical personnel, and communications. The large parking lots allowed the fleet to be parked on the grounds. Officers now had to meet at the building to exchange cars. A gas pump was put behind the facility to speed up the transfer of vehicles from one officer to another. For the police, this provided a place for roll call, locker rooms in which to change, and new cells to house prisoners.

In April 1979, the New Castle County Department of Public Safety, which included the police department, moved from the County Engineering Building into its new headquarters, the old elementary school in Minquadale. Construction (above) had to be done to the building to make it usable as a police building. This included turning the small gym into a meeting room and building a cell block. By 2003, the authorized strength of the police department was 350, and the building (below) quickly became too small. Several specialized units had to be moved off-site. After 50 years of use, the building began falling apart, with a failing infrastructure and a lack of modern amenities. The decision was made that a change had to come, and the search for a new facility began.

The land for the new building was found in the backyard of the old headquarters. In 2005, ground was broken in Minquadale on the new headquarters for the New Castle County Public Safety Building. Seen above and below, the Paul J. Sweeney Public Safety Building, with 128,000 square feet, has more than triple the space of the old building and provides the department with modern features such as specific space to analyze evidence, laboratories to examine seized computers, and a state-of-the-art operations center. Off-site police entities that had previously been housed throughout the county due to lack of space are now centralized in one building. (Above, courtesy of John Randolph.)

The New Castle County Police Department has absorbed smaller departments through its history, including the Middletown Police Department and the Brookside Police Department. As officers began patrolling south of the canal more frequently, space was needed to give the officers access to workstations. Several of the buildings used were located within the town of Middletown, including the town hall (above). Eventually, a new building was constructed to house these officers. The Southern Patrol Headquarters (below) was built in 1996 to operate as a separate entity commanded by a captain. In 2007, when the Middletown Police Department was reopened, this building became unmanned and is now used as a substation.

The New Castle County Police Academy is located in Kimberton, just outside of Newark. The 14,000-square-foot facility replaced an abandoned swimming pool in an area that experienced a high level of crime. Dedicated in 2001, the modern building (below) provides a venue for the instruction of new recruits, a community center, and a policing office. Previously, academy classes were taught at a racetrack, a community college, a National Guard base, a vacant school, and a community center (above). The academy now has a permanent home, and there is no need to be trained by outside agencies. The academy classes are open to other Delaware police agencies as well. (Below, courtesy of John Randolph.)

Carousel Park, located at 3700 Limestone Road, is the home to the New Castle County Mounted Unit. The property, originally a park, was transformed into a stable and several outbuildings (pictured), which were designed to look like the Wild West. One building includes a riding arena that is used for the extensive training the Mounted Unit conducts. This facility was used to train officers in riot control with the horses present. The facility also houses publicly boarded horses. A crew of civilians operates the facility and assists the Mounted Unit.

Recognizing the importance of officers staying in communities during shifts, the department arranged several substations throughout the county, including the two seen here. This gave officers the opportunity to write reports in the field instead of coming back to headquarters. Some of these facilities were equipped with computers prior to the officers being issued laptops. Some officers felt that typing their reports looked better, so they did so in the substations on their midnight shifts. This also gave officers a place to use facilities and eat their meals during shifts, as some facilities provided kitchen appliances for their use. Sector meetings were also frequently held at these substations because they were close to the areas in which the officers were working.

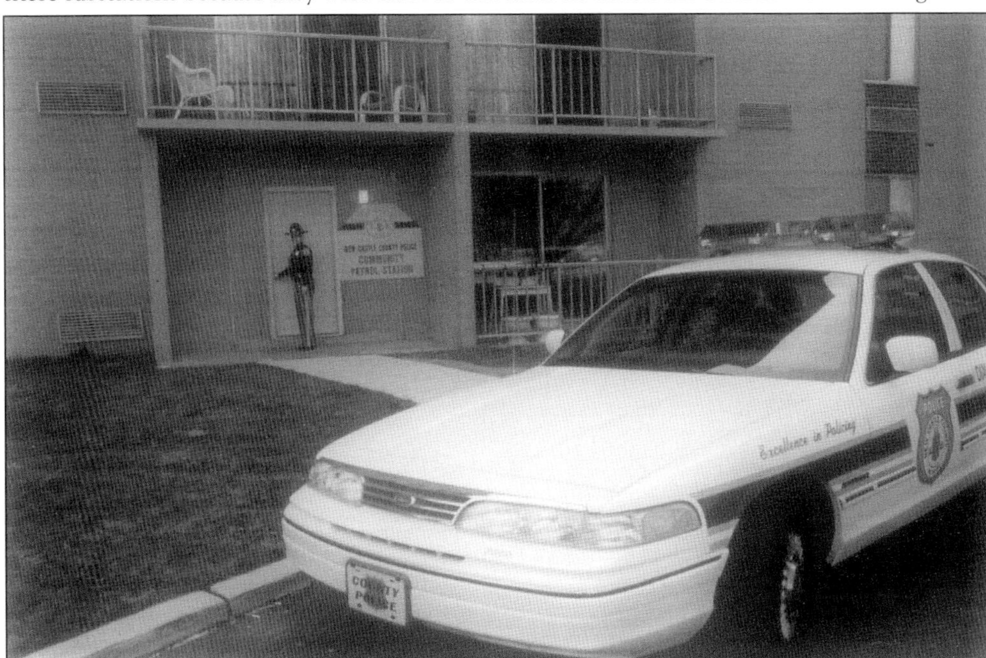

Some substations, like the ones seen here, housed entire units when the old Minquadale headquarters became too small. The Domestic Violence Unit was moved into the substation on Powder Mill Road, and the Traffic Services Unit was moved to the substation on Duncan Road. Other substations were in Canby Park Shopping Center, Edgemoor, Hockessin, Claymont, and Brookside. After the new public safety headquarters was built, many of the units in substations were moved into the new facility, leaving many of the substations unmanned. Most shut down or were sold, but a few remain open for other county programs, such as the summer camps at the Duncan Road office.

In 1977, a group of New Castle County and Wilmington police officers began construction of the pistol range. The New Castle County Police Department had received a grant from the Delaware Agency to Reduce Crime, but it was in jeopardy of losing the funds because officials were slow to identify a suitable location. From 1969 until 1972, the police department used an old banana warehouse near the Greater Wilmington Airport as an indoor shooting range. At the time, little was known about the inherent dangers of lead poisoning associated with poorly ventilated structures. When the danger became known, there was a push to find a suitable, well-ventilated location for a new range. Finally, property owned by the National Guard on Delaware Route 9 was chosen as a suitable location for the new range. This location is now utilized by several other local police agencies and has enough room for SWAT and other tactical trainings.

The range was built from the ground up by New Castle County and Wilmington police officers who possessed skills in trades such as heating and air conditioning, plumbing, and general contracting. They built everything, from the dirt berms that stopped bullets from hitting the river to the restrooms on the grounds. In 1978, the range tower was officially opened, complete with turning, pop-up, and running targets that were operated from a control tower. A ceremony was held in which citizens were invited to shoot a police-issued pistol under the watchful eyes of officers (above). A relay between officers (below) also took place.

The Police Athletic League (PAL) of Delaware was founded in 1984 by three New Castle County police officers to ensure that "the first encounter of the youth and the police officer is in a positive environment on the friendly field of sports competition." It serves to unite youth ages 8 to 18 with police officers via athletic and academic programs. Officers first began operating the program from the Edgemoor Community Center, but they soon realized that the center was bursting at the seams with the influx of youth in the area. After 10 years of fundraising and planning, the first PAL facility in Delaware (above) was finally opened in Garfield Park in 1994. This program was so successful that a second PAL (below) opened in Hockessin in March 2001.

Four

PATROL

The patrol division is the backbone of any police agency. It is the most visible of all departments, and it is usually the first contact the citizenry has with the police. Their primary duty is to respond to 911 calls 24 hours a day and 7 days a week. Other duties include routine patrol, accident investigation, the apprehension of felons, and assistance in the investigation of major crimes.

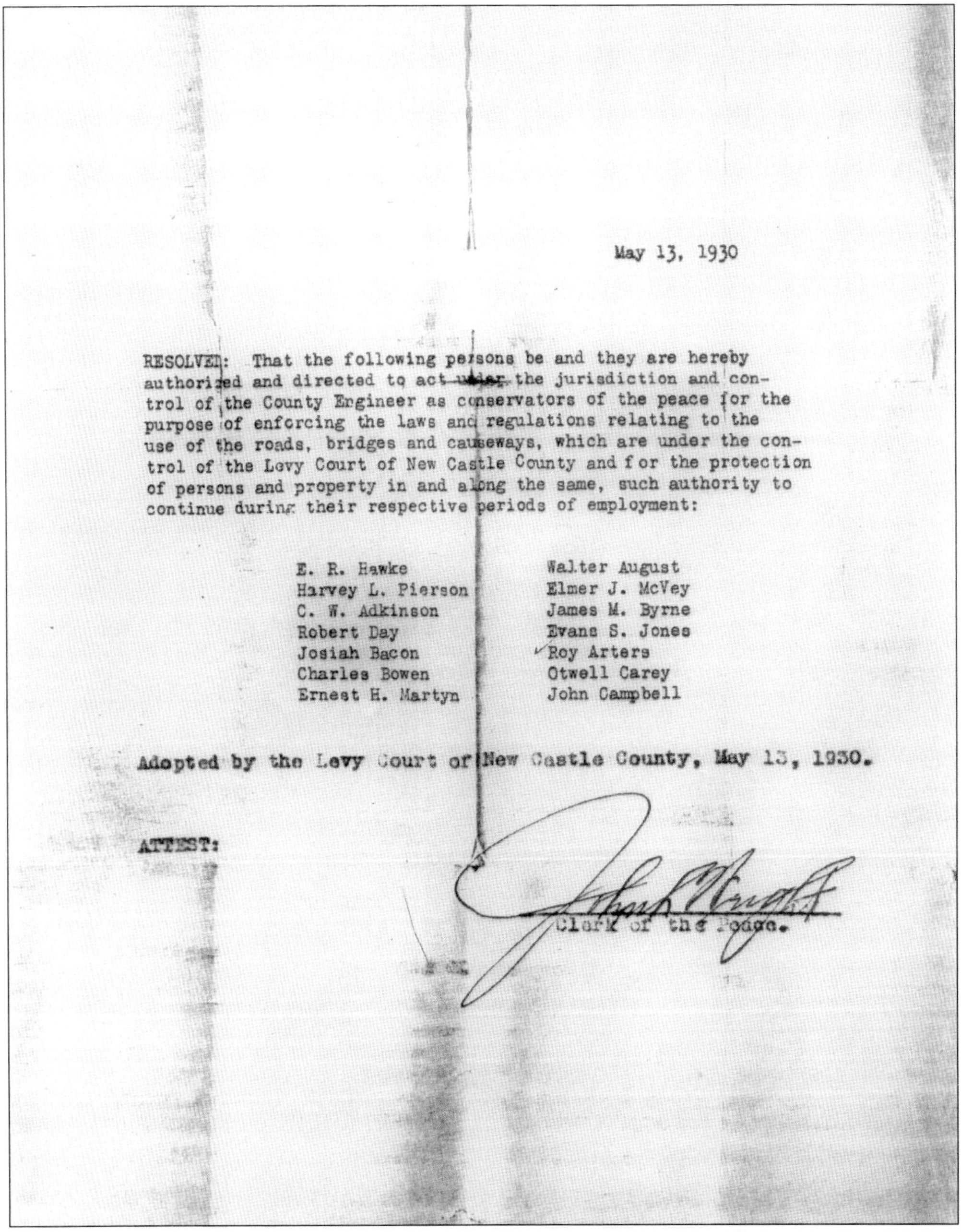

May 13, 1930

RESOLVED: That the following persons be and they are hereby authorized and directed to act under the jurisdiction and control of the County Engineer as conservators of the peace for the purpose of enforcing the laws and regulations relating to the use of the roads, bridges and causeways, which are under the control of the Levy Court of New Castle County and for the protection of persons and property in and along the same, such authority to continue during their respective periods of employment:

E. R. Hawke	Walter August
Harvey L. Pierson	Elmer J. McVey
C. W. Adkinson	James M. Byrne
Robert Day	Evans S. Jones
Josiah Bacon	Roy Arters
Charles Bowen	Otwell Carey
Ernest H. Martyn	John Campbell

Adopted by the Levy Court of New Castle County, May 13, 1930.

ATTEST:

Clerk of the Lodge.

In 1930, this resolution was passed by the Levy Court, mandating that all County Rural Police Officers attend a one-month academy. The County Rural Police continued until 1967, when it officially became the New Castle County Police Department. Col. John P. Ferguson of the Delaware State Police proposed separate jurisdictions for the county and state police departments. In June of that year, the attorney general supported the idea of separate jurisdictions. For a time, a movement to abolish the county police or merge it with the state police became prominent. A state police captain filed a report to the general assembly advocating merger or closure. Much controversy arose from the report, but due to public support, the department survived, and a jurisdictional agreement was reached in September 1970.

In April 1975, a state senator was stopped for a traffic violation by a county patrolman. Sen. J. Donald Isaacs could not provide identification, and, after a few minutes of waiting, he drove away. A felony car stop was then made by assisting officers due to the unknown nature of the incident. The second car stop initiated a legislative investigation and led the general assembly to abolish the county police under House Bill 252. The bill stripped the county police of the authority to investigate any deaths, rapes, kidnappings, or attempts to cause such crimes. After two homicide cases brought about many legal questions regarding the bill, recruits, citizens, and county employees boarded buses to Dover to show their support for the county police to remain a full-service police agency, as seen in this photograph. HB252 was repealed, and another new jurisdictional agreement was created.

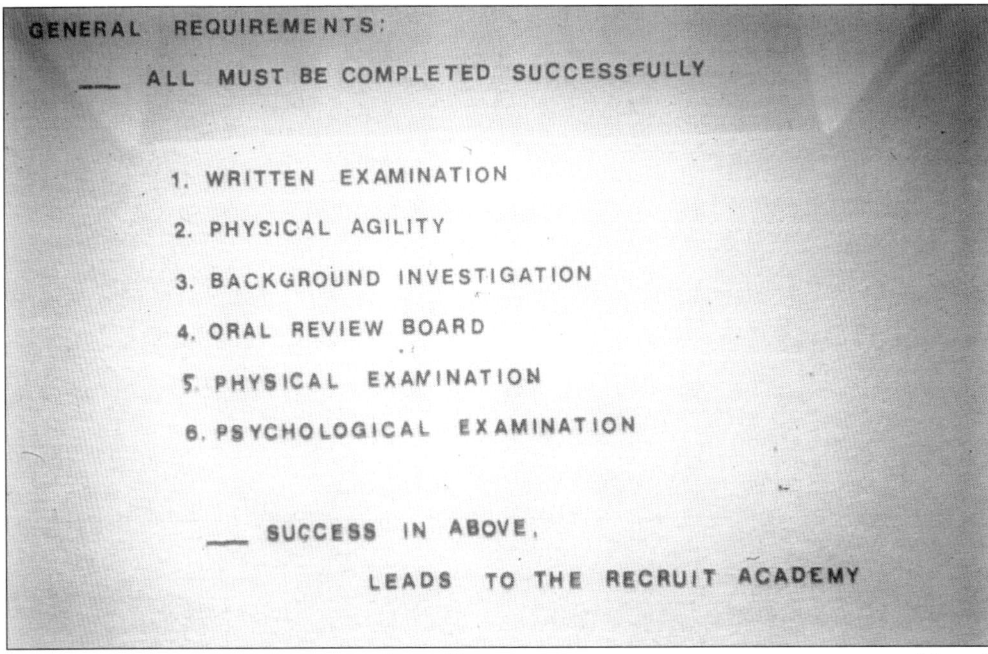

Every applicant for the position of police officer must pass a written examination, an oral board, and a physical test in order to be placed on the rolling eligibility list for one year. The physical test used to consist of push-ups, sit-ups, a wall climb, and a swim. Today, it includes push-ups, sit-ups, and a 1.5-mile timed run. Then, if a candidate is selected, the process continues with a polygraph test, psychological examinations, and an extensive background investigation. If all these tests are passed, the candidate is given an appointment at the academy. If any part of the examination is failed or if the eligibility list expires, the applicant must reapply and start the process again.

The academy lasts approximately 26 weeks. The day starts with either physical training or an inspection (right). Recruits must look sharp and polished everyday, with properly ironed clothing and polished shoes, to avoid receiving "gigs," or demerits. Physical training is not the only aspect of the academy; academics are also stressed (below). It is in this environment that recruits are taught law, policies and procedures, defensive tactics, and other day-to-day duties of a police officer. There are also shooting lessons at the range and an emergency-vehicle operations course. Days are long, usually lasting into the evening hours. All the hard work is rewarded on graduation day, when the recruit becomes an officer and receives his or her badge.

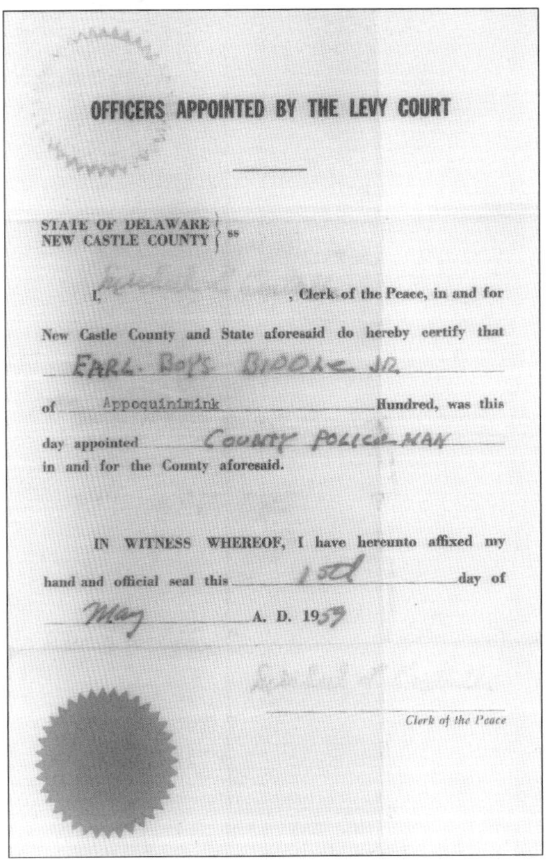

OFFICERS APPOINTED BY THE LEVY COURT

STATE OF DELAWARE
NEW CASTLE COUNTY } ss

I, ______, Clerk of the Peace, in and for New Castle County and State aforesaid do hereby certify that EARL BOYS BIDDLE JR of Appoquinimink Hundred, was this day appointed COUNTY POLICE MAN in and for the County aforesaid.

IN WITNESS WHEREOF, I have hereunto affixed my hand and official seal this 1st day of May A. D. 1959

Clerk of the Peace

Rehearsal for graduation begins several weeks before the ceremony. Many hours are spent perfecting drills and marching maneuvers. This is the special occasion that all recruits have been waiting for. Family and friends come to watch the new officers become part of the New Castle County Police Department family. Once that badge is pinned on, all of the yelling, sweating, and bleeding of the academy becomes a distant memory.

Another rite of passage is the issuance of officers' identification cards, the official representation that they are police officers. There have been several variations of the identification cards over the years, with the design, layout, and information contained on the card changing. Officers were identified by several titles over the years, including patrolman and officer, and this was reflected in their identification cards.

Roll calls are held throughout the shift to brief officers on current crime problems, departmental memorandums, and related activities, to ensure readiness for duty. Roll calls were done every day of the shift, but with the advent of technology and take-home vehicles, officers now go in service from their homes, getting briefed on new events, crime trends, and memorandums from their assigned laptops. Generally, roll calls are now held on the first and last days of the shift. Routine inspections are done on uniforms, handguns, and vehicles to ensure that the officer is prepared for duty. Command staff visits can be expected from time to time to brief the officers on important issues or to receive feedback from the officers. Roll call trainings also supplement the intense annual training officers must go through.

Until approximately 1997, officers would respond after roll call to the arms room, where a house sergeant would issue each officer a vehicle. Being a senior officer on the street was usually rewarded with the issuance of a newer vehicle. Prior to the officer's shift ending, the vehicle needed to be cleaned out and fueled before the keys were returned to the house sergeant. Prior to computers, keeping track of the vehicles was a manual effort, as illustrated in this photograph. After 1997, every officer was issued a take-home patrol car equipped with communications gear and a laptop computer, allowing constant contact with the 911 center, other patrol units, supervisors, and other emergency response units. These measures were part of the Community Enhancement Program, which aimed not just to give each officer their own car but also to increase the number of police cars in their home communities during off-duty hours. There are still frequent inspections to ensure that vehicles are maintained by the officers.

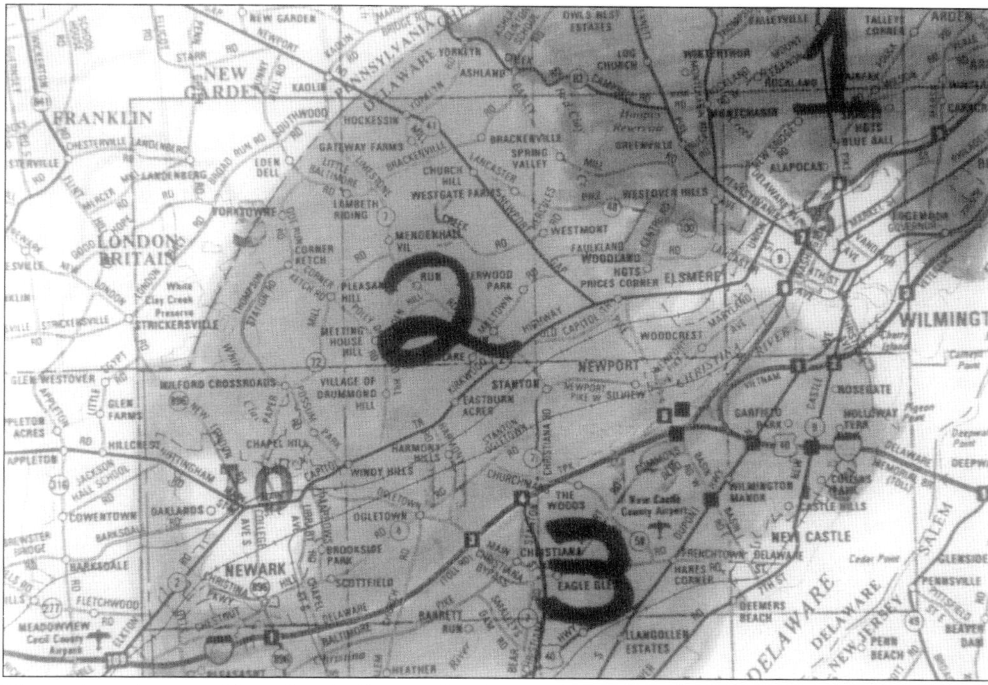

Throughout history, New Castle County has been geographically divided into many different policing districts. Currently, the county is geographically divided into four districts—northern, western, central, and southern—and each district is divided into four sectors. The patrol section is divided into five platoons, labeled A through E. These platoons overlap at peak hours, when calls for service are at their greatest. Officers work 10 hours in the day and evening shifts, and eight hours in the midnight shift. Each platoon is commanded by a lieutenant and assisted by several sergeants, who are assigned to supervise officers within the districts.

In the 1970s, after a shift was completed, the officer would drive to the oncoming officer's residence and pick him or her up. That officer would then drive the now off-duty officer home. Shifts could get lonely if one was alone. The officer at left, against regulations, brought his bulldog with him on duty. Legend has it that he was not the only one. Officers were expected to keep in touch with dispatchers and, before there were radios in cars, three officers would check in on pay phones and key boxes. Currently, officers have the luxury of in-car radios, portable radios, and cell phones. During the evening hours, county officers would routinely drive up and down community roadways with their alley lights on, lighting up homes. They wanted people to know that the county police were out and about working in the communities.

In January 1967, the Levy Court was abolished and New Castle County adopted a county council form of government, with a county executive. The new structure called for a county police department headed by a director, who was appointed by the county executive with the consent of the county council. The county police were to enforce traffic regulations and investigate accidents with the proviso that the state police be advised immediately of accidents that involved death or serious injury. The county police can make legal searches, seizures, and arrests, and maintain and operate lockups for the temporary confinement of prisoners. Officers are sworn to maintain the peace and protect life, property, and all other rights and liberties of the people, and do and perform all lawfully assigned acts. They should also operate and maintain an integrated communication system to facilitate prompt, efficient, and effective performance.

After House Bill 252, a jurisdictional agreement was made between the state police and the New Castle County Police Department to define the function and jurisdictional responsibilities of each, in order to provide improved police service in a coordinated approach to public safety. The state police have primary responsibility for patrolling and investigating requests for police service on all "major" roadways. The county police's primary responsibility is patrolling and investigating requests for police service on all other roadways. A majority of the communities were given to the county police, while a majority of the businesses and schools were given to the state police.

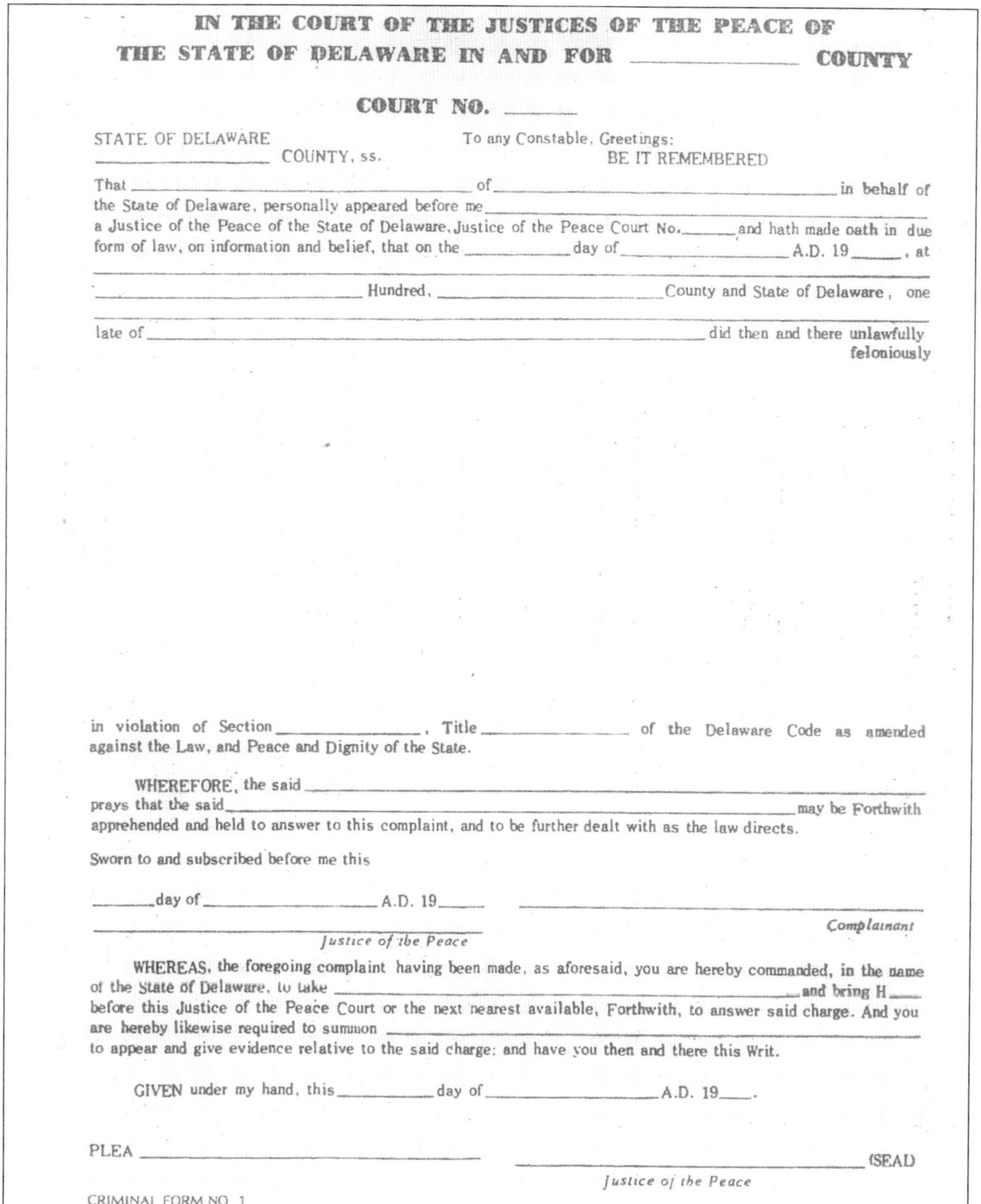

IN THE COURT OF THE JUSTICES OF THE PEACE OF
THE STATE OF DELAWARE IN AND FOR ____________ COUNTY

COURT NO. ______

STATE OF DELAWARE
____________ COUNTY, ss.

To any Constable, Greetings:
BE IT REMEMBERED

That ____________ of ____________ in behalf of the State of Delaware, personally appeared before me ____________ a Justice of the Peace of the State of Delaware, Justice of the Peace Court No. ______ and hath made oath in due form of law, on information and belief, that on the ______ day of ____________ A.D. 19______, at ____________

____________ Hundred, ____________ County and State of Delaware, one ____________

late of ____________ did then and there unlawfully feloniously

in violation of Section ____________, Title ____________ of the Delaware Code as amended against the Law, and Peace and Dignity of the State.

WHEREFORE, the said ____________ prays that the said ____________ may be Forthwith apprehended and held to answer to this complaint, and to be further dealt with as the law directs.

Sworn to and subscribed before me this

______ day of ____________ A.D. 19______ ____________

____________ *Complainant*

Justice of the Peace

WHEREAS, the foregoing complaint having been made, as aforesaid, you are hereby commanded, in the name of the State of Delaware, to take ____________ and bring H____ before this Justice of the Peace Court or the next nearest available, Forthwith, to answer said charge. And you are hereby likewise required to summon ____________ to appear and give evidence relative to the said charge: and have you then and there this Writ.

GIVEN under my hand, this ______ day of ____________ A.D. 19____.

PLEA ____________ ____________ (SEAL)

Justice of the Peace

CRIMINAL FORM NO. 1
COMPLAINT AND WARRANT

W

When a crime is detected, an arrest warrant is written. Handwritten warrants continued to be completed until desktop computers were purchased by the agency. Officers had to respond back to headquarters to type the warrants on a desktop. In 1998, the purchase of laptops allowed officers to remain in the field and complete their warrants. Officers are given discretion on certain arrest-able offenses. Community policing is a concept and philosophy that was embraced by the department in 1988. This philosophy goes hand in hand with discretion, by giving officers other options in lieu of an immediate arrest. The community policing philosophy was tested over the ensuing years and deemed a success. To effectively implement this concept, organizational structural changes were required, training had to be refocused, and deployment of assets had to be reconsidered.

The US Department of Justice described community policing thusly: "Community policing focuses on crime and social disorder through the delivery of police services that includes aspects of traditional law enforcement, as well as prevention, problem-solving, community engagement and partnerships. The community-policing model balances reactive responses to calls for service with proactive problem-solving centered on the causes of crime and disorder." After its implementation, officers were no longer just responding to reported crimes and taking reports, they were attempting to find the root of problems within the community and seeking options to change the problem by contacting citizens within the communities to assist. This is done in the form of New Castle County–sponsored community programs that provide citizens with situational awareness on burglaries, as well as child safety classes, road and traffic surveys, and trained community crime watches.

Community policing requires police and citizens to join together as partners in identifying and effectively addressing issues. Community interaction is an important aspect of an officer's duties. Proactive and tailored community methods are possible through understanding community needs and attitudes. Officers have to be ready to change their approaches to any given call. An officer can go from a barking dog complaint to a manhunt for a suspect that was shooting at police. In September 2003, due to excessive rainfall, the community of Glenville experienced devastating flooding, trapping residents inside their homes and on their roofs. Officers responded and assisted local fire companies, in boats, to recover stranded residents. Once the floodwaters receded, police were called upon to provide assistance to displaced residents and security for their property.

After a patrol officer makes an arrest, the suspect is then transported back to headquarters to await processing and arraignment. While the patrol officer is writing the warrants and conducting the investigation, assigned officers act as "turnkey officers," ensuring that the suspect is housed in a secure and safe environment until the investigation is complete. Until the late 1980s, the officer had to complete all the processing themselves, including filling out a pedigree form, taking mug shots, and fingerprinting. After warrants are obtained from the justice of the peace court, suspects are transferred to court to be arraigned. Thanks to technology, suspects no longer have to leave the building—a video arraignment system connects the cell area with a courtroom.

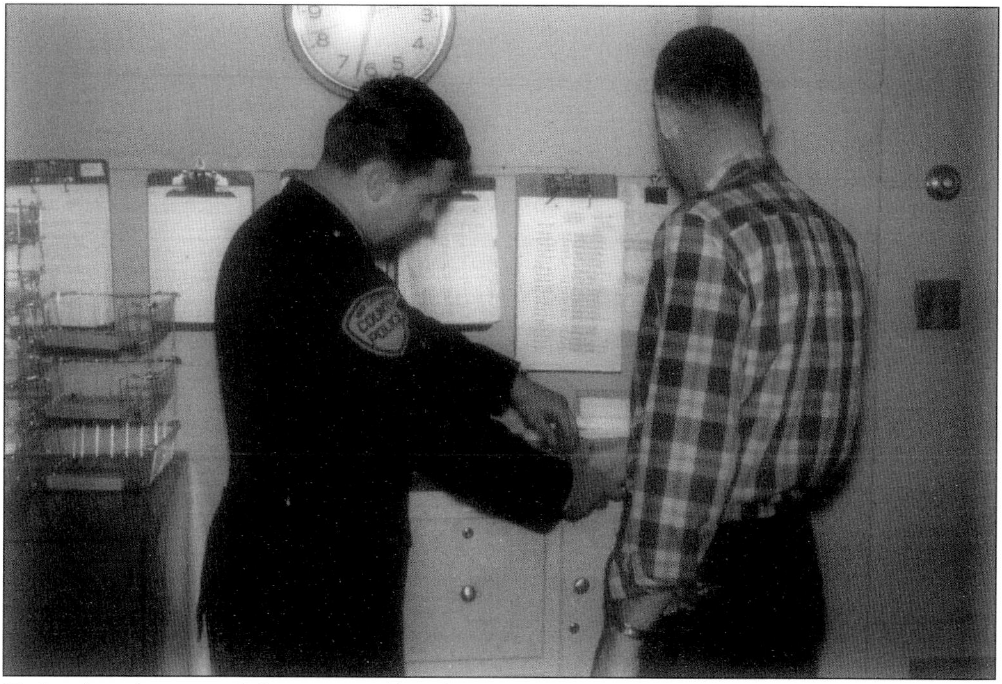

Technology has moved from manually ink-printing suspects to utilizing a program called the Automated Fingerprint Identification System (AFIS). Photographs used to be taken with a Polaroid camera and are now taken with the AFIS system. This has allowed the automation and standardization throughout the state of Delaware in regards to mug shots. Once this process is completed, suspects are either released or turned over to the custody of the Department of Corrections. Mobile AFIS units are also available in the field to assist officers in identifying suspects. This system allows instant identification, a process that used to take hours. One of these units is deployed to each platoon, and one is deployed to special operations, to ensure 24-hour coverage.

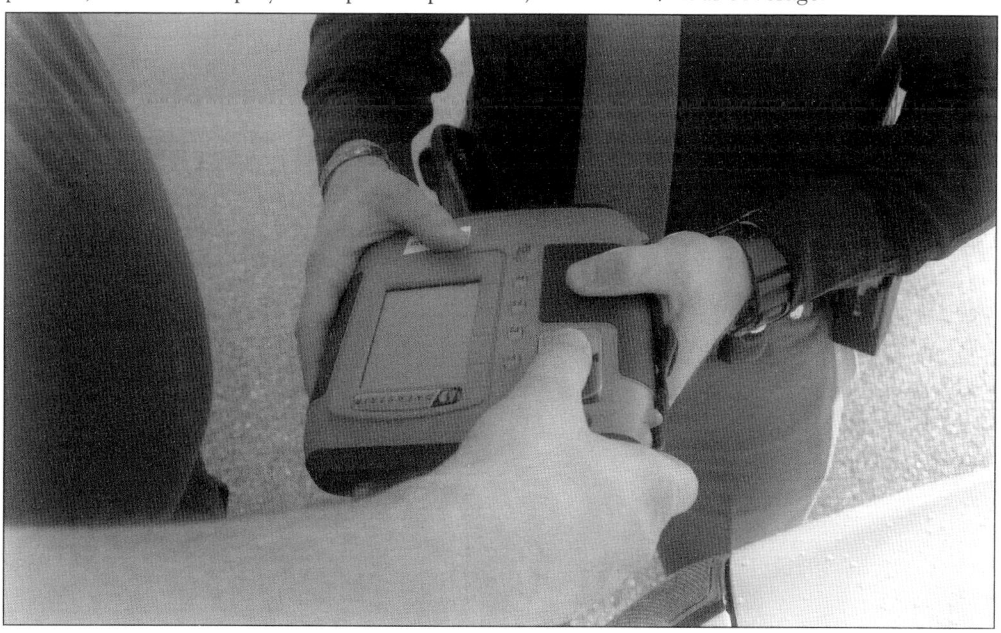

In the late 1960s and 1970s, county officers carried state police radios and answered for complaints logged by state police dispatchers. In 1971, the police communications and dispatch functions were separated from those of the fire department. When dispatch was moved from the Delaware State Police to the New Castle County Police Department, an officer dispatched the road units. Officers from both agencies sat side by side to assist responding units. In December 1980, the 911 communications center was created. In 1988, Enhanced 911 (E911) was created, especially giving caller ID to the call center. The Regional Communications Center (RECOM), staffed by civilians, is responsible for the coordination of law enforcement operations for the New Castle County Police Department and neighboring police departments in New Castle County.

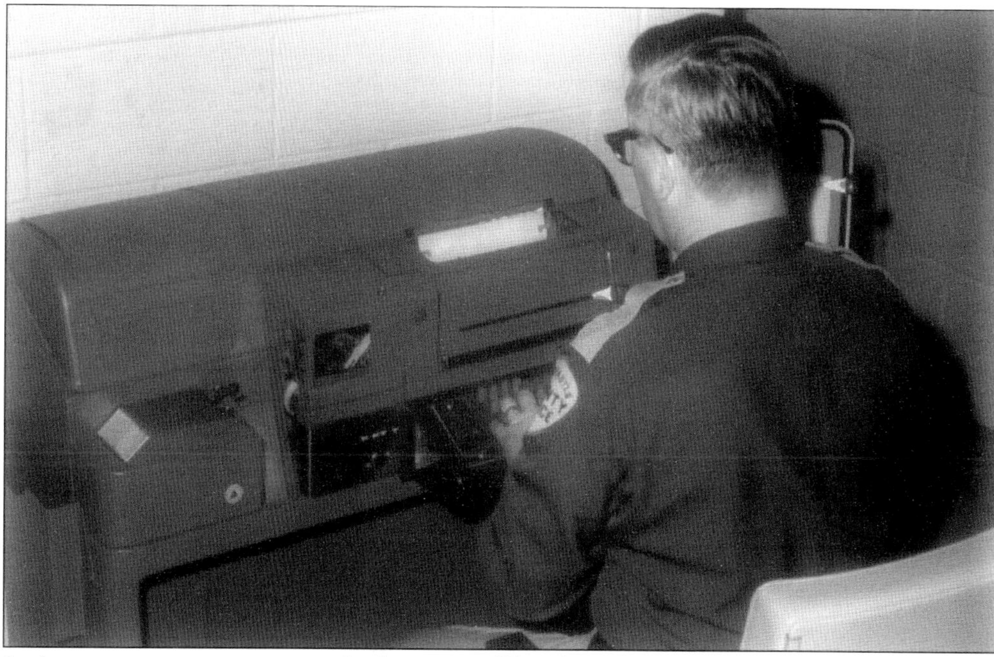

In the past, warrants, reports, and tickets were all handwritten. With the advent of the computer, the way officers performed their daily duties was forever changed. Before, registrations for vehicles had to be individually entered into a special machine, which sent the information to the State Bureau of Identification, which then ran the information and sent it back. This made running registrations tedious and time-consuming. Computers and newer programs, on the other hand, allow for instant results. Each patrol platoon is staffed with several officers trained to be "data officers," responsible for the entry and removal of warrants, stolen property, missing persons, and guns. They are also responsible for teletypes from other agencies requesting assistance.

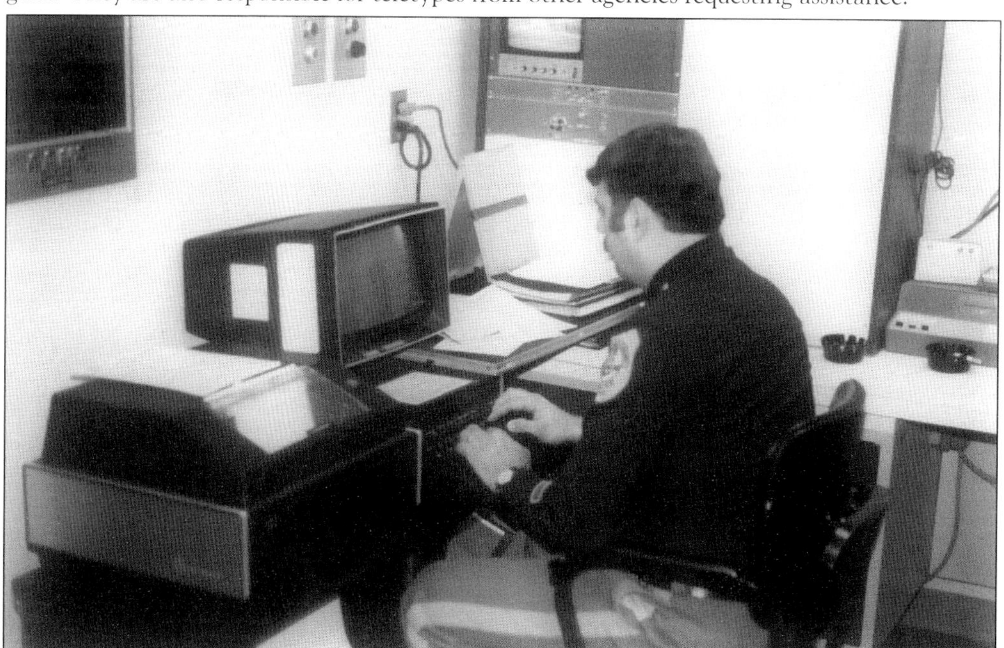

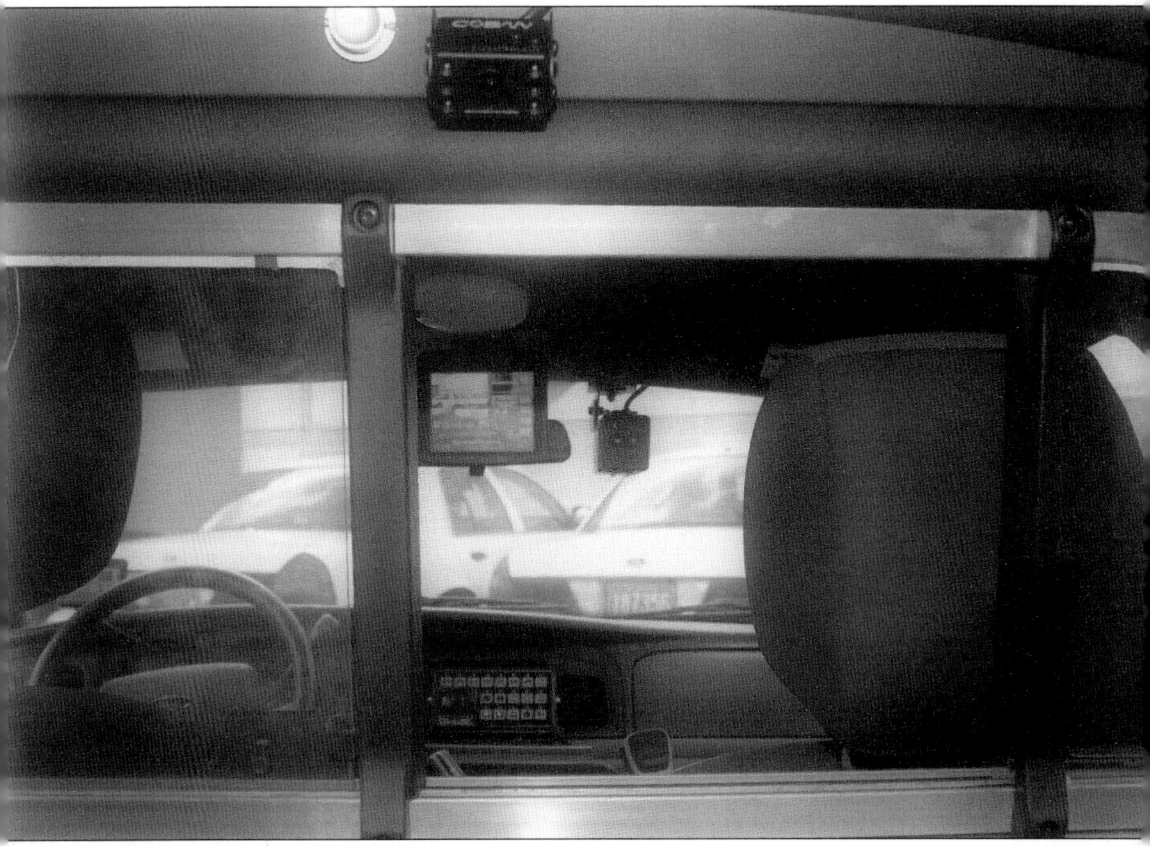

Officer safety and scrutiny are always topics of interest in the law enforcement community. Cameras were originally placed in police vehicles to document stops and activity that officers encountered. Many officers welcomed the cameras because they provided a firsthand experience for jurists and prosecutors in trial. Video allows civilians to see what the officers were experiencing at the time of the stop or encounter. This photograph shows the first camera used by the New Castle County Police Department. Technology has grown over the years; now, when an officer pulls into the parking lot of headquarters, the video from the in-car camera is automatically downloaded to server storage. Storing cumbersome DVDs and film reels is a thing of the past. The cameras now have full 1080, high-definition picture, as well as zoom capabilities. Cameras protect not only the officer but also the citizens that are served.

In 1998, Rocky II mobile computers and printers were installed in patrol vehicles. Initially, officers complained about the new computers and begged to go back to handwriting reports. The number of programs and capabilities of the laptop computer have grown over the years, and all of this technology has become a part of the daily routine of officers, who now embrace the technology available to them. Automated License Plate Readers (ALPR) have also been added to many of the vehicles in the fleet. This technology allows officers to scan vehicle registrations as they pass by a vehicle, identifying vehicles with registration violations and notifying the officer. With the possibilities available with mobile tablets, the department is currently looking to upgrade technology and possibly to replace the laptops with tablets.

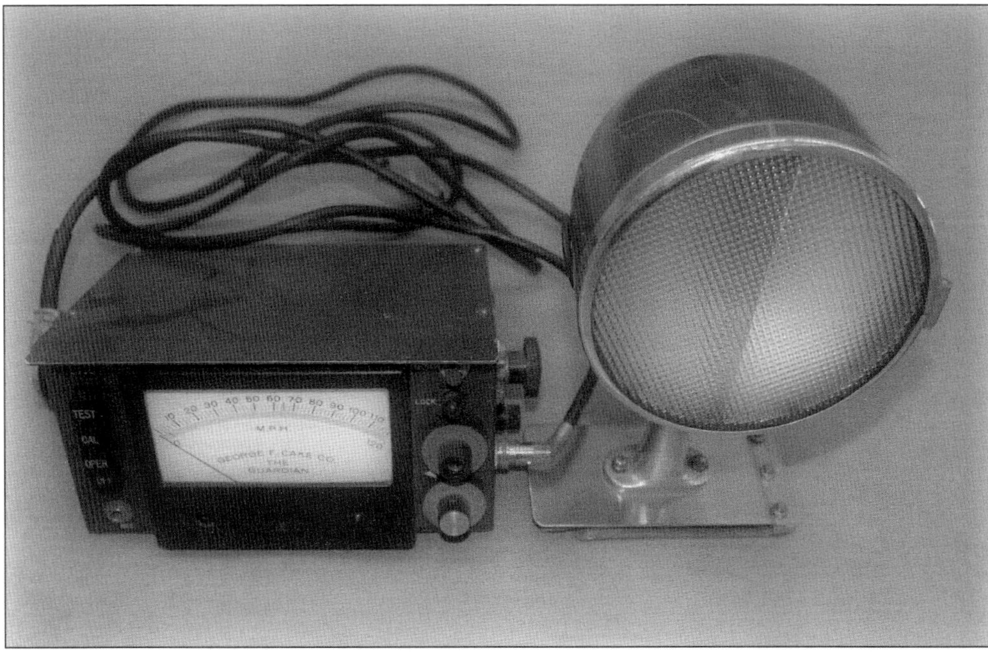

Radar units have become a very important part of policing. As with all technology, there have been huge advancements over the years. Radar has changed from being a large, cumbersome dash-mounted unit to a smaller unit that is permanently installed in the vehicles. Handheld units are also available for covert operations. The department has a Traffic Services Unit that responds to zones designated as high-violation areas. However, patrol officers are also responsible for running radar in their assigned areas to ensure the communities they police are safe. Officers must keep logs and test the equipment before and after each use.

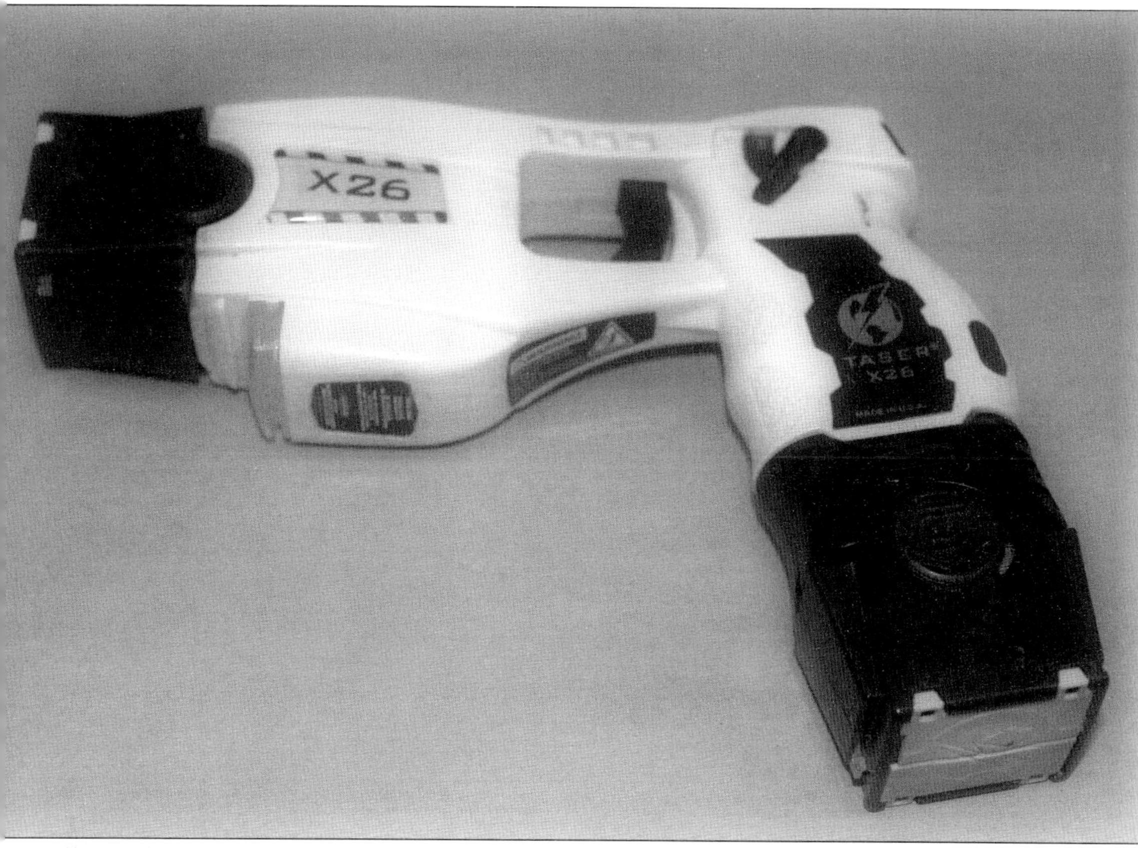

Officer safety during patrol is paramount. Stun devices have become a way for officers to safely subdue combative subjects. The first issued device was handheld, and it quickly became apparent that such close quarters were still dangerous. Engaging a combative suspect close enough to deploy the device often put officers within reach of suspects who were assaultive. The Taser, an electroshock weapon, was eventually issued to every officer. The Taser disrupts voluntary control of muscles by sending electrical current through two small dart-like electrodes that stay connected to the main device. This allows a farther distance between the combative subject and the officer, which results in fewer injuries to both. The Taser is yellow and black in color and is carried on the opposite side of the belt from the officer's firearm. This precaution keeps officers from using the wrong weapon during intense situations.

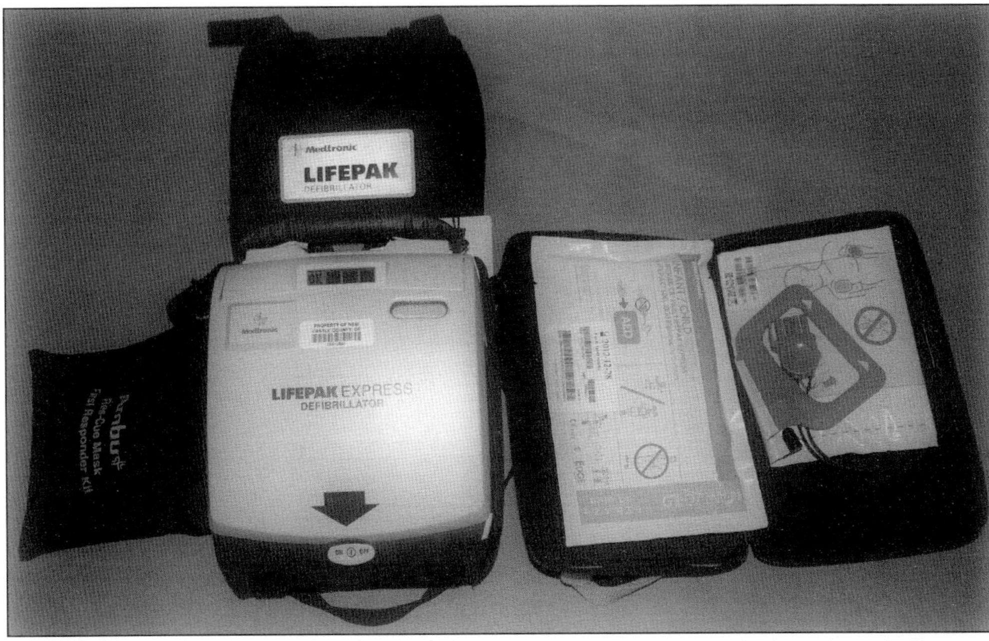

Not only is the New Castle County Police Department concerned with the safety of officers, it is also concerned with the safety, health, and welfare of the citizens it serves. A majority of the officers on patrol are issued an Automated External Defibrillator (AED). This device automatically diagnoses a potentially life-threatening cardiac episode for a patient and provides intervention for them.

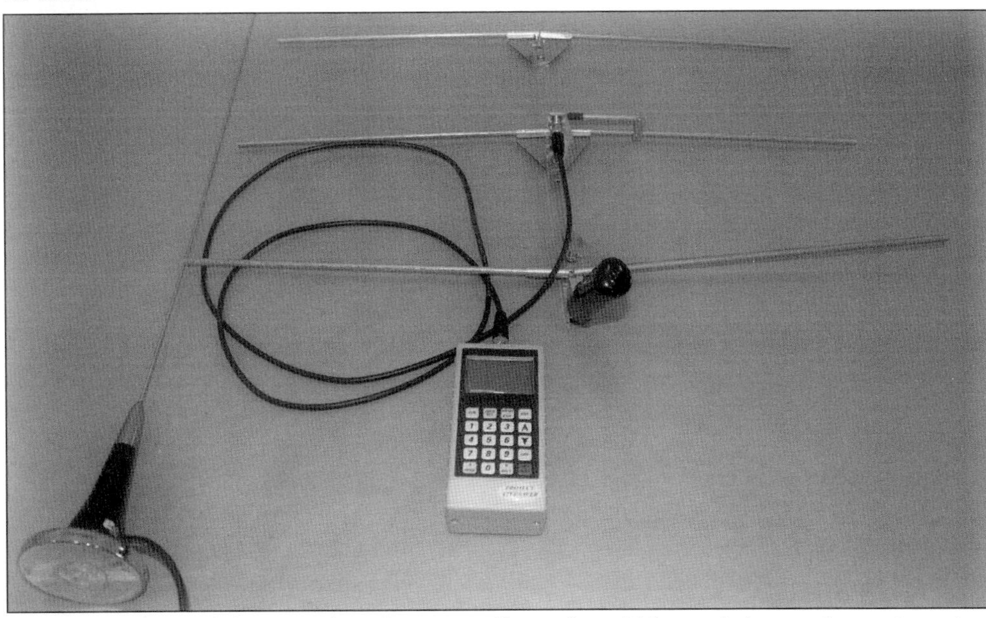

Due to an increasingly large number of citizens suffering from Alzheimer's disease, dementia, autism, Down syndrome, and other related mental disorders, the New Castle County Police invested in the Project Lifesaver Program. The program utilizes state-of-the-art technology for emergency service response to missing persons suffering from these disorders. The patient is given a device that is worn and can be tracked if he or she wanders.

The New Castle County Police Department recognizes the emotional and spiritual needs that come with the hard life of law enforcement. Father David Murphy has dedicated his service as the department's chaplain for more than 20 years. He has been there for the good and the bad, including promotional ceremonies, police memorial services, dedication ceremonies, weddings, and funerals. He has done several ride-alongs with New Castle County police officers, so he understands the job and its difficult nature. He is a recognized face at headquarters, whether in uniform, as seen in these two photographs, or in workout clothing. In 2012, he was awarded the rank of lieutenant colonel.

On October 20, 1972, Officer Paul Sweeney was seriously injured in a fiery crash on Concord Pike. He died 42 days later after a courageous battle to overcome his catastrophic injuries. He became the first New Castle County police officer killed in the line of duty. Officer Sweeney was driving north on Route 202 when his police vehicle was rear-ended. This caused the vehicle to spin into the southbound lane, where it became engulfed in flames. Officer Sweeney was treated for first-, second-, and third-degree burns over 85 percent of his body. He eventually lost his fight, and passed away on November 30, 1972. Sweeney was known for his endless quest to reduce and recover stolen vehicles in the communities. He was posthumously promoted to the rank of corporal, and the Paul J. Sweeney Public Safety Building was named in his honor.

On September 16, 2011, Sgt. Joseph Szczerba responded to a 911 call for a disorderly subject. Upon arrival, Sergeant Szczerba located the possible subject and attempted to detain him, at which time a foot pursuit ensued. Sergeant Szczerba was able to catch up to the subject, and a violent struggle took place, during which Sergeant Szczerba was stabbed and fatally wounded. The subject was arrested and charged accordingly. Szczerba was known for being a "cop's cop" and a hands-on supervisor. He was posthumously promoted to lieutenant a few days after his death, and was awarded the Police Medal of Honor. The New Castle County Police Academy has since been named in his honor.

The New Castle County Police Department constantly strives to be a leading force in the law enforcement community, always searching for new technologies and concepts to combat crime. The citizens are a vital part of the reduction of crime, and their knowledge of their own communities is invaluable. The department continues to keep officers in the communities, and they speak with residents as often as possible, but calls for service can make this a tough task. Crime has been significantly reduced over the years; however, the department is battling new hurdles as technology has also made criminals more advanced. Patrol officers are the front line and are responsible for the primary investigation of all crimes. However, there are many times when the scope of an investigation requires additional resources and training that can be provided by specialized units.

Five

SPECIALIZED UNITS

The idea of special units came about when police departments realized that many factors contribute to crime, including economics, lack of alternatives, and less police presence in communities. The New Castle County Police Department developed several units to prevent, intervene, and solve crimes that occur within their jurisdiction, and often assists other agencies to solve crime as well. The Mounted Unit is pictured here.

The Criminal Investigations Section is comprised of several units, or squads, that are staffed with specially trained investigators. They are responsible for the investigation of major crimes, ranging from burglary to homicide. Among their achievements are the conviction of Delaware's first serial killer, Steven Pennell, who was responsible for the deaths of five females, as well as the apprehension of Delaware's first serial rapists, Michael Siple and Kevin Howard, who were responsible for the rape of more than 20 women. Different units within this section have detectives that specialize in the specific investigations that they are assigned to. The Family Services Unit ensures a coordinated response to cases involving children, such as child abuse and neglect, sexual exploitation, and homicides. The Megan's Law/Sex Offenders detective is responsible for notifying the community of the presence of offenders.

Missing Persons' primary responsibility is locating missing persons and juvenile runaways. The Persons Unit is responsible for investigating homicides, deaths of a suspicious nature, serious assaults, robberies, hate crimes, kidnappings, and extortion. The Property Unit is responsible for identifying and investigating crime trends and problems related to burglaries, thefts, and criminal mischiefs. The Criminal Analysis Unit maintains a crime and suspect database to facilitate analysis, and produces reports on crime series, patterns, trends, and offenders to aid in the identification, arrest, and prosecution of criminals. A newer unit, High Tech Crimes, investigates computer-based crimes, including child pornography and fraud investigations. All the units under the Criminal Investigative Section use a variety of techniques and technologies to help them solve crime. This includes surveillance, computer programs, interviewing skills, community contact, and patrol support.

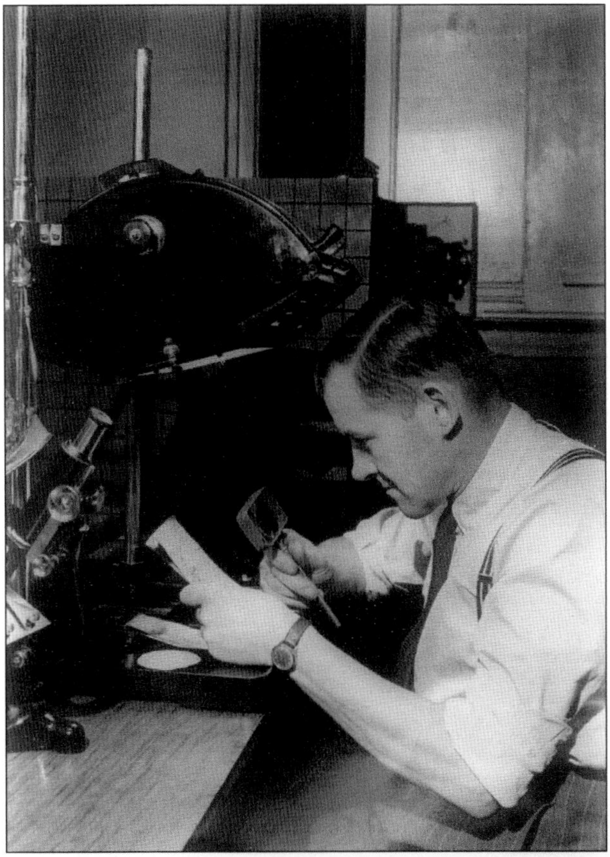

The Evidence and Detection Unit is responsible for the processing of crime scenes, which can range from collecting and analyzing evidence to documenting a crime scene through photographs, video, and sketches. At one point, cameras with film were used to document scenes. Now, there is technology that allows a machine to scan a room and create a computerized scene reproduction. This unit responds to several different scenes, including death investigations, burglaries, robberies, and major assaults. When cases of gun violence occur, the unit is generally called out to collect the evidence, including firearms. Firearms-related evidence is entered into the Integrated Ballistic Information System, maintained by the federal Bureau of Alcohol, Tobacco and Firearms (ATF). Death-related investigations usually result in an autopsy, where a member of this unit will respond to document the findings.

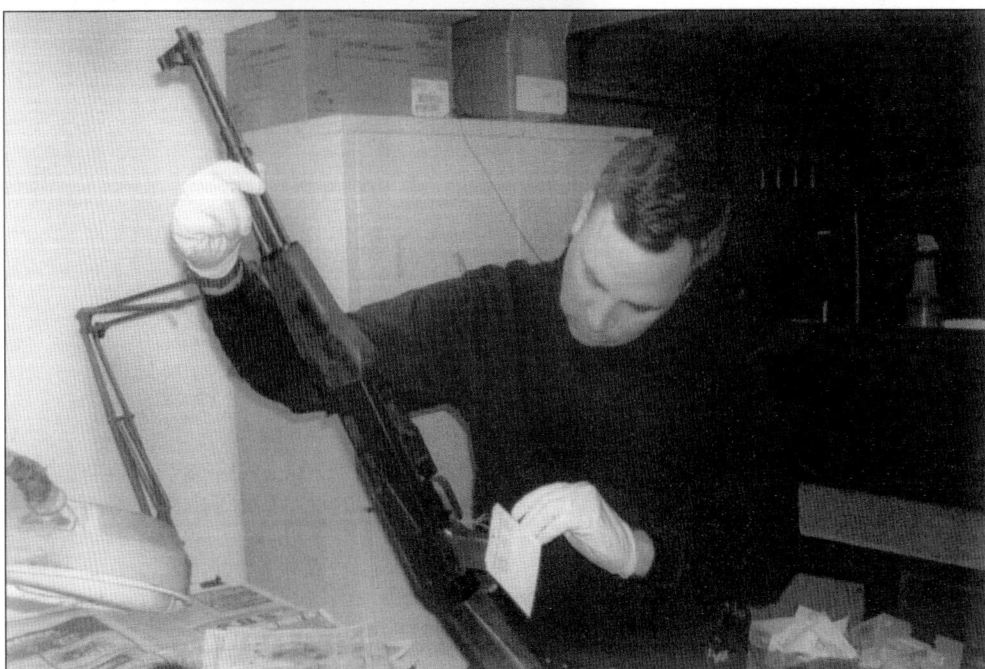

Another duty that is frequently performed is fingerprinting. Comparing fingerprints used to be done manually, utilizing magnifying glasses. Now, the collected prints are entered into the Automated Fingerprint Scanning system for comparison to prints on file. The system then stores the prints for comparison later if a match is not made. Members of the unit go through extensive training to keep their skills and knowledge of evidence-collecting current. Training includes fingerprinting, photography, and even a trip to the "body farm," which allows members to view bodies that have been donated in several stages of decomposition, in order to educate them on the process.

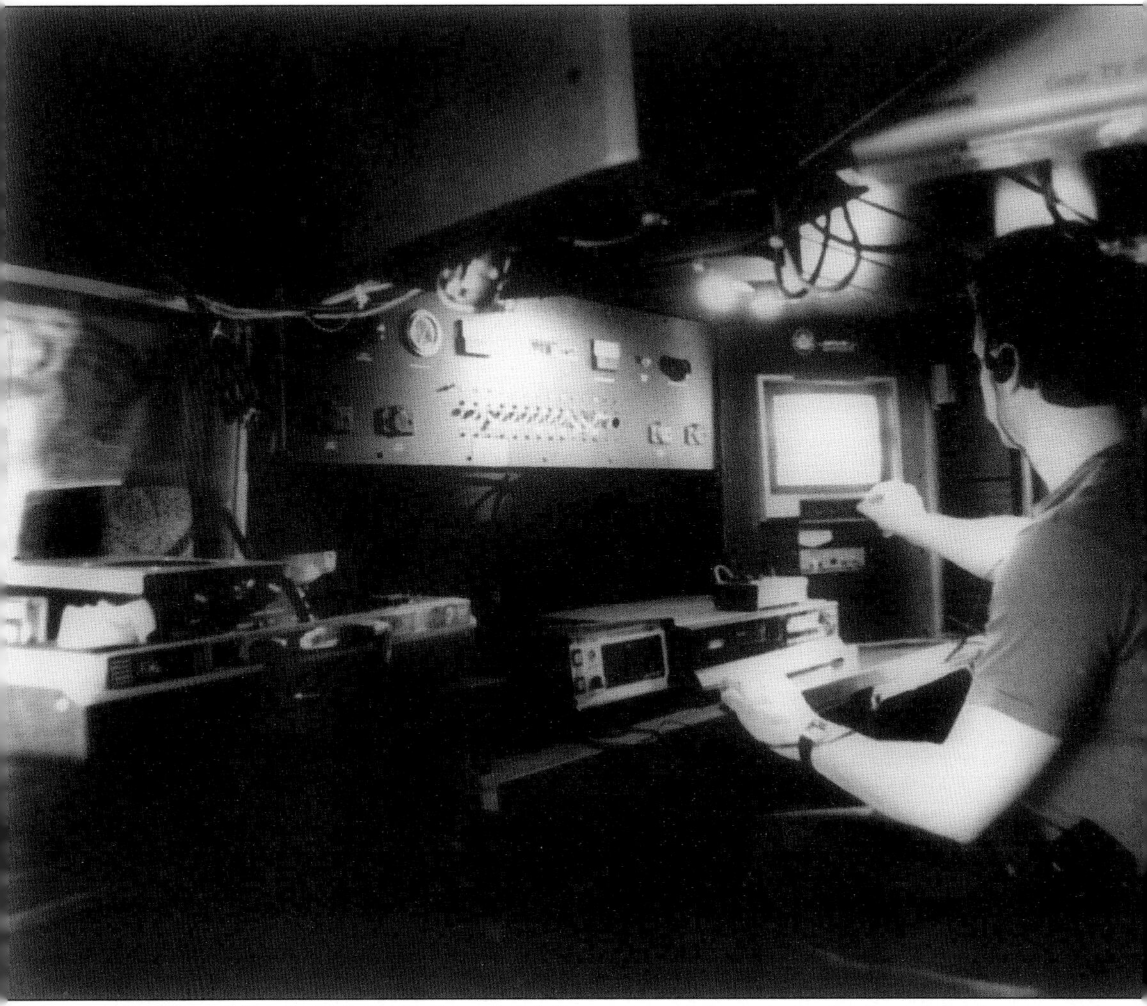

The "Drug Unit," which has had several different names through the history of the department, is responsible for identifying and investigating drug trends and other problems in communities, and then providing solutions and actions to combat them. Cases involving drug activity are ascertained from citizen complaints, information from informants, information from patrol officers, and complaints from community representatives. Over the years, the unit has been responsible for the seizure of drugs, money, vehicles, and other assets pertaining to crime. The unit's other responsibilities include conducting surveillance for other units within the organization by identifying and locating suspects wanted for other crimes, as well as drug-related offenses. One method of surveillance is the use of vehicles equipped with cameras and computers. This allows for the documentation of crime as it occurs and provides evidence that is used in court proceedings and prosecutions. A Drug Unit member is pictured doing surveillance.

The Special Weapons and Tactics (SWAT) team is supervised by the special operations commander. The team is on-call 24 hours a day and 7 days a week. The SWAT Unit is responsible for the logistics and deployment of special equipment needed during critical incidents and works with all elements of the police department.

They also investigate complaints that pertain to acts of lewdness, prostitution, patronizing a prostitute, and promoting and permitting prostitution. This is done through several different uses of technology, including surveillance, wiretaps, informants, and undercover work. This team utilized different weapons and breaching tools.

The SWAT team responds to the most complex and dangerous situations that officers can face, including felony warrant attempts, high-risk search warrants, and barricaded subjects. Each member receives specialized training in advanced tactics and weapons, hostage rescue, repelling, and warrant service. The team has been used for protection details for several dignitaries, including presidents, vice presidents, and senators. In 1998, the team was awarded honorable mention at the Top Cops awards ceremony held by the National Association of Police Organizations in Washington, DC. The award was for a 48-hour barricade of a resident in Raven Glen, which ended in the apprehension of the subject after the SWAT team deployed a distraction tactic and then rushed the subject while he was near the roadway and outside the residence. The entire operation was completed without the loss of life. (Courtesy of Retired Senior Cpl. George Bell.)

The Crisis Negotiation team is called upon to resolve critical incidents, which include but are not limited to hostage/barricaded situations and suicidal persons. In every hostage/barricade incident, it is the primary goal of the Crisis Negotiation team to resolve the crisis without violence. The crisis negotiator's primary responsibility is to establish communications with the adversary and develop a positive dialogue to bring the situation to a successful and peaceful conclusion. The duty of the Crisis Negotiation team is to ensure the safety of any hostages, innocent persons, and police officers, and to apprehend the subject without injury, unless it is unavoidable. This task is completed by several highly trained and motivated officers, who are team-oriented and work together to coordinate resources and speak to subjects during standoffs and other situations. They perform well under pressure, possess good communication skills, are in good physical condition and sound mental health, and are always willing to report for duty with little or no notice.

The crisis negotiators work hard in their attempt to resolve all crisis situations through timely negotiations, which will give a subject in crisis the opportunity to rationally assess the situation and provide negotiators time to formulate a plan of action to successfully resolve the incident. This team works closely with the SWAT team and has had overwhelming success on several different investigations. Negotiators have to attend an extensive training program and work on negotiating scenes before they are allowed to be active negotiators with subjects. The team trains once a month and has grown over the years. It is always reaching out to other agencies within the tristate area, in the hopes of training together. The goal is for the teams to work soundly with one another in case there is a multi-jurisdictional incident. Several training operations have been conducted with role players from area colleges as well as other law enforcement officers.

The Explosive Ordnance Disposal (EOD) team conducts the investigation, storage, and safe destruction of all explosive and suspicious devices. The team responds to improvised explosive devices, vehicle-borne improvised explosive devices, booby traps, military ordnance, suspicious packages, fireworks, and all other types of explosive, hazardous, and dangerous materials. It is also responsible for the safe removal and destruction of any devices found. It conducts post-blast crime scene investigations, assists the Evidence Detection Unit with the collection and preservation of evidence, and provides technical support to the Special Operation teams. The team also assists other police agencies in the area. The members of the team are on an on-call basis, and must be able to respond to a scene quickly and assess the need for the rest of the team to respond out. If the team is needed, the additional members are notified and respond.

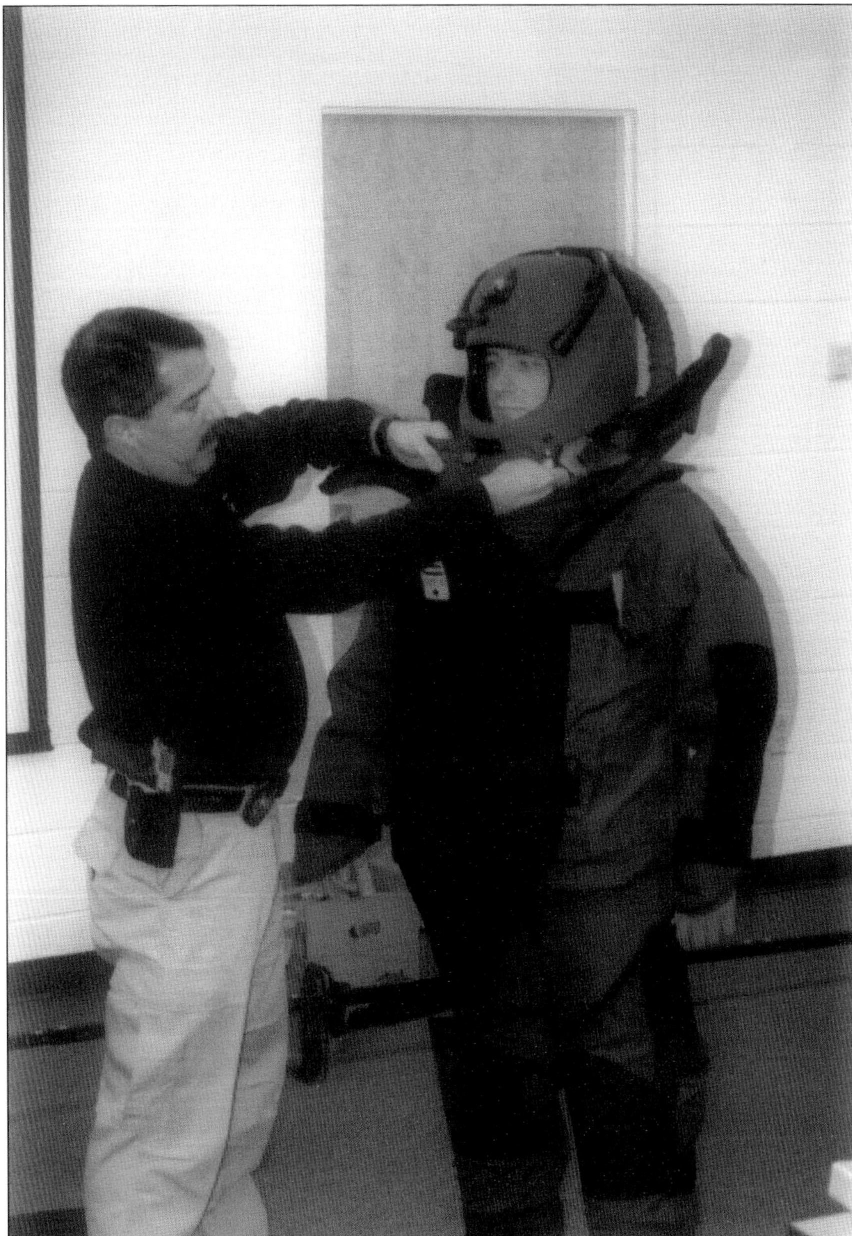

Each officer assigned to the EOD team must attend the FBI's Hazardous Devices School for basic bomb technician certification, and then return every three years to maintain certification. Technology has assisted the EOD team in the disruption and destruction of potential hazardous items. Robots and other devices have been acquired by the New Castle County Police Department to keep its officers and EDO specialists at a safe distance while assessing and dealing with potential threats. The officers are equipped with special bomb suits that help shield them from possible lethal blasts that may deploy while they are working hands-on with an explosive. Here, an EDO technician has a recruit try on the suit in order to appreciate the limited mobility and protection it has to officer. Every officer is taught what the EOD team's job is, and how to respond to potential hazards before the EOD team arrives.

The Scuba team was assembled when the need for underwater evidence recovery was discovered. The original team consisted of four New Castle County police officers. All the officers had personally obtained scuba certification and had their own equipment. The team trained for underwater vehicle submersions and evidence recovery. Once, a burglary investigation led the team to a pond to search for a safe that was stolen. The team was deployed and the safe was recovered. Due to the lack of available training time, the team was eventually shut down. Today, boats and other technologies are utilized in water operations for the recovery of evidence. (Below, courtesy of Sgt. Richard Dunning.)

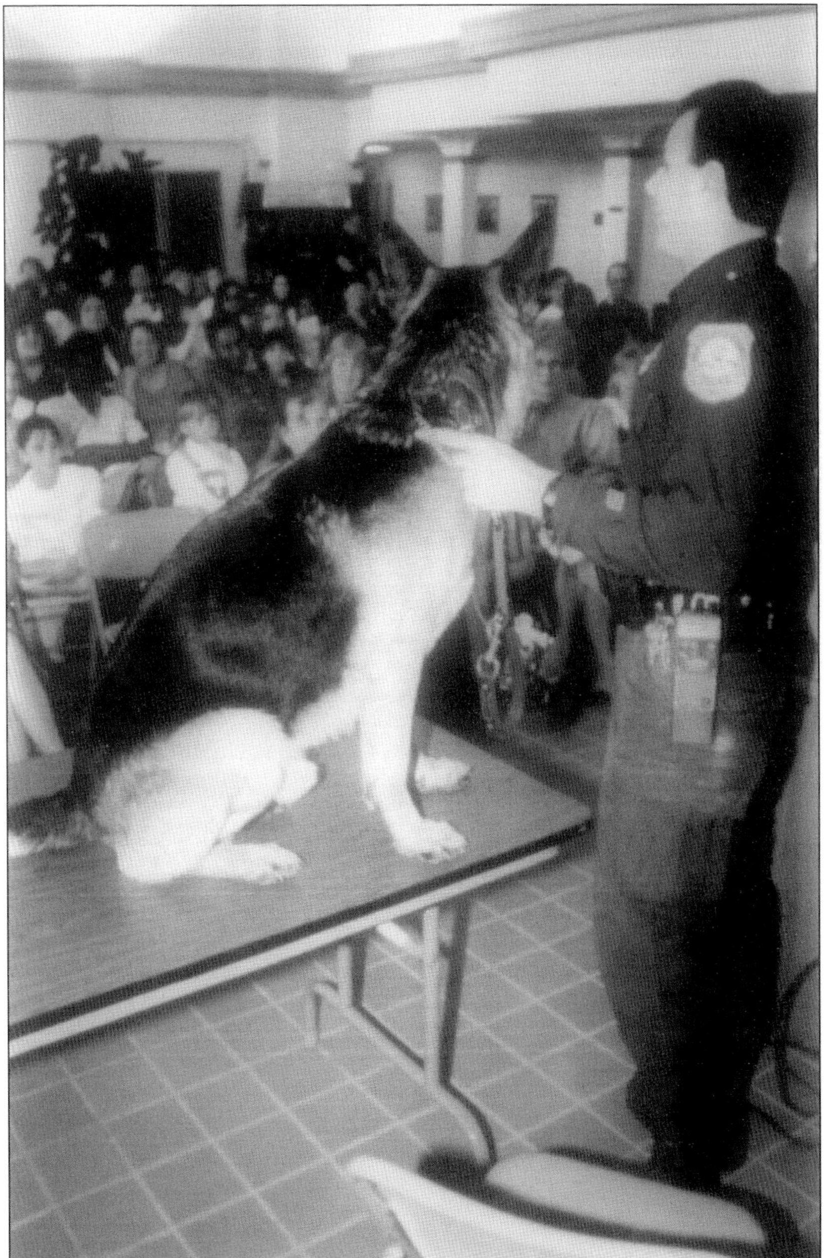

The Canine Unit was started in 1986 with one officer and a bloodhound named Jesse, who was only trained to track subjects. Today, there are more than 10 teams engaged in search and patrol work. Training takes 12 to 21 weeks, with each dog cross-trained to perform searches for contraband, missing persons, and routine patrol work. Each patrol unit has a canine unit assigned to it. The objective of the Canine Unit is to provide support to personnel within the division with a highly mobile, specially trained police canine team. The canines greatly enhance the department's capabilities in locating persons and items related to the investigatory process. Several breeds have been used, including Bloodhounds, Labradors, German and Dutch Shepherds, Malinois, and mixtures of these breeds.

Each canine handler strives to ensure that all citizens view the New Castle County Police Canine Unit as an essential part of the community, involved in providing a better quality of life for its citizens, through interactions such as events and school presentations and reducing crime in the community. The unit has its share of heroes, including Nero, who saved the life of his handler after knocking the gun out of a robbery suspect's hand. After 10 years on the force, Nero was forced to retire, with a record of seizing over $1 million in drug, cash, and property. He also earned numerous commendations for merit and valor. (Right, courtesy of Officer First Class Stephen Donahue.)

In October 1981, the county council passed a plan to add the Mounted Patrol Unit to the force, with a 4-2 vote. The original plan included a start-up price tag of $121,000—the funds that were needed to purchase and board eight horses, two pickup trucks with trailers, and build new stalls at the Wilmington Police Stables. This was only possible with a grant from the Community Development and Housing (CD&H) program, which wanted to have a police presence in some of the communities that it funds. Several different breeds of horses have been used by the unit, but the community favorites are the Clydesdales, who are known as "gentle giants" and are noted for their intelligence, good temperament, and excellent qualities for police horses.

Training for the Mounted Unit is extensive, and the unit is highly competitive, regularly participating in national competitions throughout the United States. The unit has taken first place in several divisions through the years. The unit patrols communities and county parks, targeting the communities in need of special patrols. It also provides security details and represents the police department at special events. Residents can also see the unit running radar from the horses within the communities. The New Castle County Police Department is currently looking into the purchase of tablets and mobile printers for the unit, so tickets can be issued right from the saddle.

The Motorcycle Patrol and the Bicycle Unit are specialized units created to provide a police response in situations involving different terrain, or in cases where there are traffic impediments to a response. They also provide a heightened police presence in the community and foster greater interaction between the police and local residents. They can be deployed in specific cases where their capabilities are required, or for longer-term service in a community experiencing unusual crime activity. Officers must attend hours of specialized training for both the motorcycle and bicycle units in order to be able to operate them in an official police capacity. Since the inception of the motorcycle division, only Harley-Davidson motorcycles have been used. For the past several years, the unit has been used often to escort dignitaries, including senators and Delaware native Vice Pres. Joe Biden. New Castle County Police bicycles and motorcycles also regularly take part in several parades throughout New Castle County.

The New Castle Parks Unit responded to calls for police service and was responsible for special events in county parks. There are more than 500 parks in the county's jurisdiction, consisting of approximately 10,000 acres. The rugged terrain of the parks required officers to operate four-wheel-drive and all-terrain vehicles for patrol functions. The park officers planned and organized the security and safety for all special events in parks throughout the year, including Sleep Under the Stars at Carousel Park. The high visibility of the patrol enabled citizens to enjoy a safe visit to county parks. The number of reported crimes in parks is at an all-time low since the inception of the unit. Due to a shortage of officers on patrol, this unit was eventually dissolved to enable more officers to respond to 911 calls throughout the county.

The Traffic Services Unit supports the department through investigating, serving as a training resource, providing additional staffing when needed, and augmenting patrol-level traffic enforcement daily. The unit investigates and reconstructs all accidents involving a fatality or serious injury, or when a departmental vehicle is involved in an accident with injuries. All other collisions are investigated by patrol, or by a supervisor if it is departmental. The unit includes trained personnel who use a computer-aided program to recreate the scene of an accident. The Optimus GPS survey system, for measuring and recording on-scene data and preparing collection diagrams, is one example of equipment used by the unit. In 2003, the unit began to start integrating digital photography into the investigation and reconstruction process.

Traffic and accident data is analyzed and provided to other departmental personnel to enable the effective deployment of officers. The unit is also responsible for training officers in accident investigation, the use of radar, and enforcement of driving under the influence laws. Traffic services officers are also trained in truck enforcement. These officers develop and participate in traffic safety programs for the public, including a "Mocktails" presentation, in which citizens put on a set of goggles that blur their vision to simulate being intoxicated and are then asked to perform tasks. This unit is also active with the New Castle County multi-jurisdictional DUI Checkpoint Strike Force.

A Christmas food drive coordinated by officers in the late 1920s is seen above. Even though the department was considered the Highway Patrol at the time, these officers were the beginning of "community policing." In 1976, the Crime Prevention Unit (later the Community Services Unit), whose vehicle is seen below, was established. The challenge was to reach out to the community using nontraditional policing techniques to educate the public on crime prevention. The six-officer unit concentrated on such topics as burglary prevention, residential security, and crime-prevention checks. In March 1989, Capt. Thomas P. Gordon was appointed chief of police. During his term, the Community Services Unit, which had already been operational for more than 10 years, became more proactive. Gordon is credited with making the New Castle County Police Department a premier law enforcement agency, advancing the agency not only in community policing but also in technology.

The department's Community Services Unit had officers assigned and working in every community in the county. New programs were also started, including the Citizen's Academy, the Drug Abuse Reduction Education program (DARE), and the Gang Resistance and Education Training (GREAT) program in the schools south of the canal. These programs give children a realistic view of life after gang involvement and drug use, and provide strategies to resist these vices through fun and education. Safety Town was also created, in which officers and civilians would teach children road and sign safety in a small simulated town complete with mock houses, streets, and bicycles that children used to learn the rules of the road. Reaching out to children early in life has always been an important goal of the department. McGruff the Crime Dog, seen here, is a children's favorite who teaches about crime.

Today, the Community Services Unit offers more than 35 programs to the public upon request. These programs run the gauntlet from watch programs (community, block, child, radio, realtor) to safety programs (personal, child, senior citizen, bicycle, driving, holiday, gun, vacation, pool, Halloween). Prevention programs for rape and assault, driving under the influence, and carjacking are also provided. The Community Services Unit currently operates and oversees several vibrant, continuing programs. A senior outreach program was also developed. Senior Rollcall is an automated telephone reassurance program that calls senior citizens on a daily basis. Failure to get a response will result in attempts to notify relatives or neighbors, or, if necessary, initiate a police response.

The Heroin Alert Program dates back to 1998, after an investigative team of police officers and paramedics discovered a marked increase in the use of heroin and a ready supply from the Philadelphia area. A program was developed that gives attendees a graphic, hard-hitting, shocking presentation designed to capture the attention of the audience and leave a lasting impression. By the end of 2004, the program had been seen by nearly 700,000 citizens in the tristate area, and it continues today. The Community Services Unit recently added a Latin American Community Center liaison. The officer's primary function involves daily communication with the Latin American Community Center and the coordination of its day-to-day operations related to crime prevention in Spanish-speaking communities. The New Castle County Police Department recognizes that a language barrier should not stop outreach programs, so several programs are translated and presented to different communities.

The Youth Police Academy is a program offered to juveniles that abbreviates, yet mirrors, the police academy. The program is conducted annually with youngsters ages 12 to 15 who have an interest in exploring careers in law enforcement. The program offers campers hands-on instruction taught by experienced members of the department. The intent of the program is not only to educate participants in police work but also to foster a positive relationship with the youth in the community. The program consists of physical training, familiarization with the New Castle County Police Department's specialized units and patrol, firearms safety and shooting lessons, and a trip to the National Law Enforcement Officers Memorial in Washington, DC. The Community Services Unit also offers a Citizens Academy for adults.

The Police Athletic League (PAL) of Delaware prides itself on being an integral part of the lives of young people. Throughout the school year, as well as in the summer months, the PAL offers many different prevention programs that aim to deter juvenile delinquency. The officers' presence and influence on the young people promotes a positive outlook for their possible future endeavors. The mission of the PAL is to prevent youth crime in Delaware by providing youth between the ages of 8 and 18 with supervised athletic, educational, and social-development activities. The PAL reaches out to youth with programs that encourage community participation and address citizenship, self-esteem, substance abuse, and respect for law and order. Future vice president Joe Biden is seen here at a PAL event when he was a US senator representing Delaware.

The PAL offers several activities for children, including baseball, basketball, flag football, karate, and wrestling. Middle school dances are also often held at the centers, to give children a place to go on Friday nights. Here, karate lessons are being led by police officers, who enjoy these activities on their off-time. They bring their talents and skills to the PAL to teach kids new activities that keeps them off the streets and away from crime. There is an officer assigned to each PAL for children to interact and participate with. The goal of these officers is to impact the children's lives in a positive way and offer them a facility they feel safe to come to visit. Children find that interaction with uniformed law enforcement officers who participate with them leaves a positive impression of police and facilitates an open environment.

The honor guard is a ceremonial unit composed of selected officers. This unit is reserved for officers who are highly motivated, maintain exceptionally high standards of appearance and conduct, and show aptitude for ceremonial duty. Primary duties of the honor guard include providing funeral honors for fallen comrades and serving as the "guardians of the colors," displaying and escorting the national, state, and New Castle County flags on ceremonial occasions such as graduations. The unit wears the Class A uniform, which includes a blouse coat. Members also wear a gold aiguillette, or shoulder cord, over their left shoulders. (Below, courtesy of Cpl. Jennifer Bunora.)

The media coordinator's office prepares press releases to inform the public of upcoming events related to the police department and to report criminal activity in the community. The office also interfaces with members of the press and broadcast media, responding to their questions on departmental matters. Through a cooperative relationship with the media, the office facilitates the dissemination of timely and accurate information on matters of public interest. The New Castle County Division of Police actively seeks to establish a cooperative climate in which the news media may obtain information on matters of public interest in a manner that does not hamper police operations. However, certain information must be withheld from the news media in order to protect the constitutional rights of an accused person and to avoid interference in departmental investigations.

The Evidence and Supply Unit receives, catalogs, and stores all evidence acquired in the investigation of a crime. The unit provides security and control of seized, recovered, and evidentiary property, as well as abandoned, lost, or found property in the custody of the agency. This is critically important in supporting investigations, helping to guarantee successful prosecutions at criminal and civil trials, facilitating the timely return of property to its rightful owners, and establishing the department's reputation as an honest, reputable agency worthy of the public's confidence and trust. Ultimate disposal of evidence is done in accordance with state law. The unit is also responsible for the issue and maintenance of uniforms and equipment to officers. These areas are restricted to most officers in order to maintain accurate supply counts and ensure the safety of evidence.

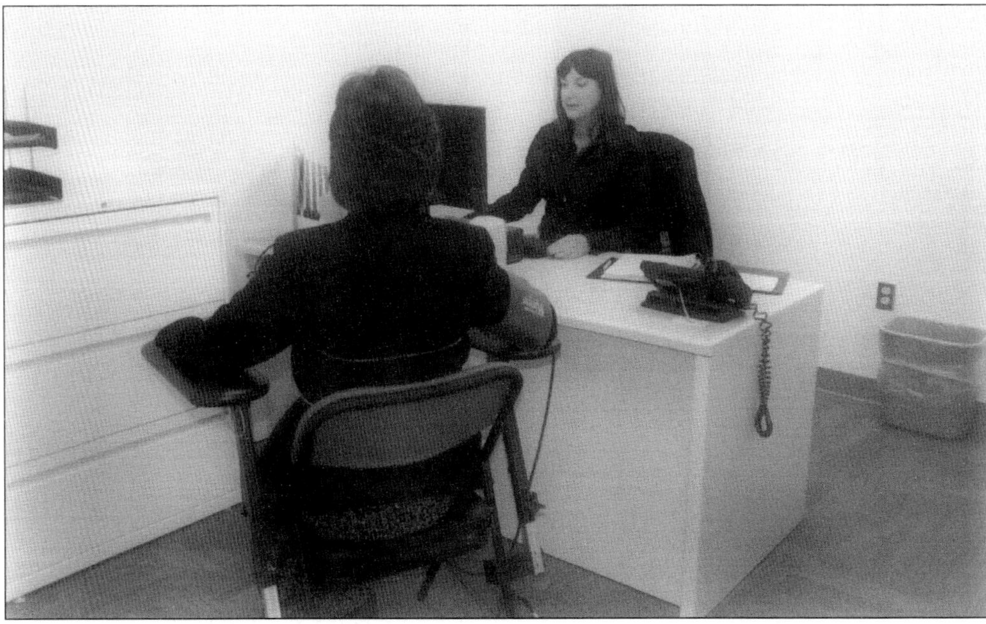

The Professional Development Unit is tasked with the hiring and training of new police officers and the in-service training of existing officers. The unit is required to provide 16 hours of training per year for every officer, but the average amount of training given is about 40 hours. The unit regularly seeks out progressive and reputable police training programs nationwide, and procures necessary funding as well as travel and lodging for officers to attend. The unit reviews hundreds of applicants and assists through the hiring process. They conduct the written examination, coordinate oral boards, schedule psychological and medical exams, and administer polygraph examinations.

The Professional Development Unit also provides the staff for the police academy, which consists of a sergeant and an officer. Additional officers are brought in to assist the staff throughout the academy. The staff is responsible for creating an academy curriculum and arranging for qualified instructors to present the necessary training specified by the Council of Police Training (COPT). The academy is a quasi-military program that provides an environment for recruits to learn in. Academy staff also ensures the recruits are physically in shape by doing daily physical training. In 1999, the 25th New Castle County Police Academy graduated the largest class in the history of the police department, with a complement of 41 officers.

The Records Unit maintains the department's record management system, which interfaces with the statewide Law Enforcement Information Support System (LEISS). The unit properly and accurately maintains all records of the department, and also logs and distributes subpoenas to officers to ensure their appearance for any hearings or court appearances.

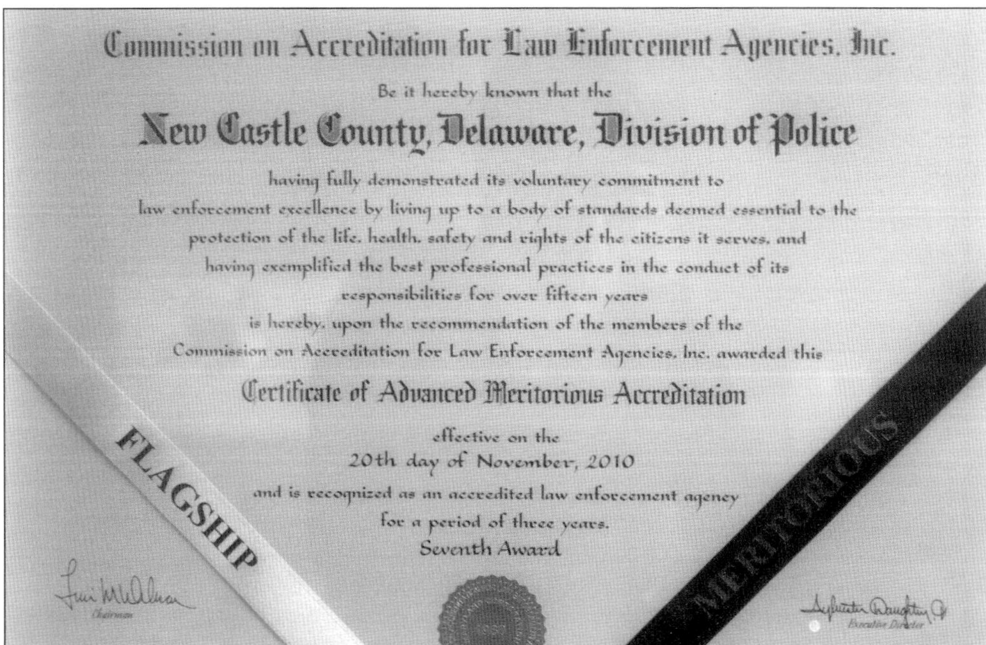

The Research, Development and Inspections Unit is responsible for researching new and innovative approaches to police work, developing departmental policy, and ensuring compliance with accreditation standards. The department is one of the few agencies in the nation with 100-percent compliance to mandatory and optional standards. In 2011, the New Castle County Police Department was recognized as a Commission on Accreditation of Law Enforcement Agencies (CALEA) flagship agency.

As the New Castle County Police Department heads toward the future, the past is never forgotten. The memories of the officers who have come before will never be forgotten, the excellence of the officers serving now is recognized daily, and the vision of the department for future officers is hopeful. The duty of a police officer is a calling, a career, and a lifestyle that is not to be taken lightly. Law enforcement officers sacrifice daily to keep the communities they serve safe, sometimes at the final expense of their lives. The New Castle County Police Department will never forget those who gave the ultimate sacrifice in the service of others. While their deaths will never be forgotten, it is their lives of service that will never be forgotten, and which forever put the citizens of New Castle County in their debt. This is the National Law Enforcement Officers Memorial located in Washington, DC. All law enforcement officers who have been killed in the line of duty from across the United States are memorialized on this wall. (Courtesy of Retired Cpl. John Krzyiack.)